WORLD WAR III: NORDIC FORCES

FINNISH, SWEDISH, NORWEGIAN, & DANISH FORCES IN WORLD WAR III

Written by: Wayne Turner
Editors: Peter Simunovich, John-Paul Brisigotti
Graphic Design: Casey Davies, Victor Pesch
Miniatures Design: Evan Allen, Tim Adcock, Matt Bickley, Will Jayne
Cover Art and Illustrations: Vincent Wai
Miniatures Painting: Jeremy Painter, Victor Pesch, Aaron Te Hira-Mathie, Wayne Turner

Additional Writing by: Antti Arajärvi, Michael McSwiney, Garry Wait, Mitch Reed
Proof Readers: David Adlam, Antti Arajarvi, Jason Berkan, Tom Culpepper, Mark Goddard, Alan Graham, Jacob Hopkins, Lance Mathew, Michael McSwiney, Gavin van Rossum, Richard Steer, Jeff Stehr, Garry Wait, Andrew Willis, Daniel Wilson
Playtest Groups: M.E.G. Team Voghera/Cavalieri dell-Esagono (Giacomo Gotter/Livio Tonazzo), Flames Of War Regina Rifles (Lance Mathew), Aylesbury Wargames Club (Alan Graham), Brisbane Rebel Dropbears (Garry Wait)

CONTENTS

NATO's Northern Flank 2
 World War III in Scandinavia 4

Finnish Forces in World War III 7
Kapteeni Heikkilä's Jääkäri Company 10
Finnish Force 12
 Finnish Special Rules 13
 NATO Allied Support 13
T-72FM1 Armoured Company 14
 T-72FM1 Armoured Company 15
 T-72FM1 Armoured Platoon 15
T-72FM2 Armoured Company 16
 T-72FM2 Armoured Company 17
 T-72FM2 Armoured Platoon 17
T-55M Armoured Company 18
 T-55M Armoured Company 19
 T-55M Armoured Platoon 19
BMP-1 Jääkäri Company 20
 BMP-1 Jääkäri Company 21
 BMP-1 Jääkäri Platoon 22
 81mm Mortar Platoon 22
 BMP-2 Jääkäri Platoon 23
 120mm Mortar Platoon 23
BTR-60 Jääkäri Company 24
 BTR-60 Jääkäri Company 25
 BTR-60 Jääkäri Platoon 26
 95 S 58-61 Anti-tank Platoon 26
Finnish Support Units 27
 BM-21 Hail Rocket Launcher Battery . 27
 2S1 Carnation Howitzer Battery 27
 BMP-1 OP Forward Observer 27
 T-55 Marksman Anti-aircraft Platoon . 28
 ZSU-57-2 Anti-aircraft Platoon 28
 ITO 78 Anti-aircraft Missile Platoon . 29
 PstOhj Anti-tank Missile Platoon 29
 BMP-2 Recon Platoon 29
Finnish Basing and Painting 30
Finnish Catalogue 32

Swedish Forces in World War III 36
Persson's Centurions 38
Swedish Force 40
 NATO Allied Support 41
 Swedish Special Rules 41
Strv 103 S-Tank Tank Company . . . 42
 Strv 103 S-Tank Tank Company 43
 Strv-103 S-Tank Tank Platoon 43
Strv 104 Centurion Tank Company 44
 Strv 104 Centurion Tank Company . . 45
 Strv 104 Centurion Tank Platoon . . . 45
Armoured Rifle Company 46
 Pbv 302 Armoured Rifle Company . . 48
 Pbv 302 Armoured Rifle Platoon 49
 Ikv 91 Tracked Anti-tank Platoon . . . 50
 Pvrbv 551 Anti-tank Missile Platoon 50
 Pbv 302 Armoured Recon Platoon . . . 51
 Pvpjtgb RBS Anti-tank Missile Platoon 51
 Pvpjtgb 90mm Anti-tank Platoon . . . 51
Swedish Support 52
 Bandkanon 1 Armoured Howitzer Battery 52
 Epbv 3022 Forward Observer 52
 Lvrbv 701 Anti-aircraft Missile Platoon 53
 HkP 9 Helicopter Platoon 53
 AJ 37 Viggen Attack Group 53
Swedish Basing and Painting 54
Swedish Catalogue 56

Norwegian Forces in World War III 60
Brigaden i Nord-Norge 63
Gundersen's Stridsvogneskadron . . . 64
Norwegian Force 66
 Norwegian Special Rules 66
 NATO Allied Support 67
Leopard 1 Tank Squadron 68
 Leopard 1 Tank Squadron 69
 Leopard 1 Tank Troop 69
M113 Storm Squadron 70
 M113 Storm Squadron 71
 M113 Storm Troop 72
 NM142 Anti-tank Troop 73
 M125 81mm Mortar Troop 74
 M106 107mm Mortar Troop 74
Norwegian Support Units 75
 Feltvogn (TOW) Anti-tank Section . . 75
 NM195 Air Defence Battery 75
 M109 Field Artillery Battery 76
 M113 OP Forward Observer 76
 Feltvogn Recon Troop 77
 NM135 Recon Troop 77
 AV-8 Harrier Attack Flight 77
Norwegian Basing and Painting . . . 78
Norwegian & Danish Catalogue . . . 80

Danish Forces in World War III 84
Jyske Division 87
Ansgar's Panserinfanteri 88
Danish Force 92
 Danish Special Rules 92
 NATO Allied Support 93
Danish Tank Squadrons 96
 Leopard 1 Tank Squadron 96
 Leopard 1 Tank Platoon 96
 Centurion DK Tank Squadron 97
 Centurion DK Tank Platoon 97
Armoured Infantry Company 98
 M113 Armoured Infantry Company . 99
 M113 Armoured Infantry Platoon . . 100
 M125 Mortar Platoon 101
 M106 120mm Mortar Platoon 101
 M113 TOW Platoon 101
Danish Support Units 102
 Centurion Tank-hunter Platoon 102
 Redeye Air Defence Group 102
 M109 SP Howitzer Battery 103
 M113 OP Forward Observer 103
 Scout Group 104
 Tornado Strike Flight 104
Danish Basing and Painting 105
Scenarios 107
 On the Frontier Scenario 108
 Hold and Flank Scenario 110
 Mountain Pass Scenario 112

NATO AND WARSAW PACT DEPLOYMENT AND PLANNED WARSAW PACT ATTACKS ON THE CENTRAL FRONT

USSR
(UNION OF SOVIET SOCIALIST REPUBLICS)

Helsingin Sanomat
Monday, 5 August 1985:

Helsinki: The Finnish Prime Minister has expressed their concerns to the Soviet ambassador over the increasing military activity along their border. The Prime Minister has sought assurances that the Soviet Union will not violate Finnish sovereignty during this time of crisis. No representative of the Soviet embassy was available for comment.

TV-ohjelma 1 News
Wednesday, 7 August 1985:

Breaking: Despite repeated reassurances that Finland's territorial sovereignty would not be breached, Soviet troops crossed the border today. Soviet forces have attacked into Lapland in the north, and into the provinces of Kymenlaakso, South Karelia, and North Karelia in the south. In an address to the nation the President has stated Finland will not bow to bullying, especially to allow an attack on a fellow Nordic nation, and that Finland will strongly resist this attack. The foreign minister has flown to Stockholm today for urgent talks with their Swedish counterpart and the NATO Secretary General.

Verdens Gang
Tuesday, 6 August 1985:

Soviet Build-up on the Border

Oslo: NATO forces continue to resist Warsaw Pact attacks across West Germany's eastern border, but several thrusts have broken through on the north German plain, threatening Bremen and the Netherlands. Meanwhile, Soviet activity in the Norwegian Sea on the northern border near Kirkenes has dramatically increased and mobilised Norwegian forces have been preparing for and expect an attack. It is understood further NATO troops will reinforce northern Norway.

Aftenposten
Thursday, 8 August 1985:

Sweden is at War

Stockholm: Sweden has joined the fight against Soviet aggression. Yesterday the government strongly protested the Soviet Union's breach of Finland's neutrality and declared Sweden's support of Finland, both militarily and politically. The military has been fully mobilised and aircraft have already been sent to support Finnish forces.

CNN Delayed Report
Monday, 12 August 1985:

Here in Copenhagen there is much uncertainty. Locals follow what reports are available on the fighting in Jutland, watching with concern as the Danish and West German troops are pushed further north with each passing hour. Many fear the Warsaw Pact will make an amphibious landing on Zealand any day now. Danish troops are on high alert all across the Danish islands. Just in this area alone I've seen a number of prepared positions manned by Danish troops, grim-faced and watchful as they wait to see what comes next.

World War III: Team Yankee

IT'S 1985 AND THE COLD WAR JUST GOT HOT!

World War III: Team Yankee is a complete set of rules for playing World War III Wargames. You will command your troops in miniature on a realistic battlefield.

Originally based on the book written by Harold Coyle in 1987, Team Yankee brought the conflict that simmered throughout the Cold War to life.

In Team Yankee, a heavy combat team of M1 Abrams tanks and M113 armoured personnel carriers faces a Soviet invasion of West Germany. Outnumbered and outgunned, Captain Sean Bannon and his men will have to fight hard and they'll have to fight smart if they are going to survive.

Lt. Colonel Yuri Potecknov's motor rifle battalion is preparing to execute its mission in the scientific manner that he had been taught at the Frunze Military Academy and used in Afghanistan. Victory today will bring the world proletarian revolution that much closer.

Find out more at:

www.TEAM-YANKEE.com

All rights reserved. No part of this publication may be reproduced, stored in a retrieval system, or transmitted, in any form or by any means without the prior written permission of the publisher, nor be otherwise circulated in any form of binding or cover other than that in which it is published and without a similar condition being imposed on the subsequent purchaser.

© Copyright Battlefront Miniatures Ltd., 2023. ISBN: 9781988558387

CENTRAL FRONT

BALTIC SEA

The end of World War II left all of the Nordic countries critically aware of their defensive interests. Norway and Denmark had been unprepared for the German invasions, so after the war they were early members of NATO. They quickly went about rebuilding and reorganising their defensive forces. Sweden had remained neutral throughout the war, but had built up its armed forces during it to counter the possible threat from either Germany or the Soviet Union. Sweden maintained its neutral stance during the Cold War, establishing powerful air, ground and coastal forces, while maintaining good relations with the west.

Finland had seen Soviet aggression up close, losing territory, having to adhere to military restrictions, and being forced into neutrality after their armistice with the Soviets in 1944. The Finns maintained outwardly friendly relations with the Soviet Union, but remained wary of Soviet intentions and directed most of their defensive measures towards their eastern neighbour, although they never officially acknowledged such a position.

KEY

Armoured Divisions
Each symbol represents a division
Armoured divisions contain between 200 and 350 tanks and 11,000 and 20,000 troops.

Mechanised Divisions
Mechanised divisions contain between 50 and 220 tanks and 13,000 and 20,000 troops.

NATO FORCES
- United States
- Great Britain & ANZAC
- West Germany
- Belgium & The Netherlands
- France
- Canada

WARSAW PACT FORCES
- Soviet Union
- Czechoslovakia
- East Germany
- Poland

THE COLD WAR

WORLD WAR III IN SCANDINAVIA

Global tension between the West and the Soviet-led block eventually brought about war, with Soviet and Warsaw Pact troops crossing the inner German border on 4 August 1985.

Negotiations between the Soviet Union and Finland during the months before the war's outbreak had failed to secure the forces of the Soviet Leningrad Military District free passage through Finland's northern Lapland region towards Sweden and Norway. After this rebuff the Soviet staff quickly made adjustments to their plans for the capture of Norway. They decided not to limit their attack on Norway to the narrow Norwegian-Soviet border with accompanying naval landings, but to attack across a wider front though Finnish Lapland. The key objectives of their offensive would be to secure Norwegian airfields and ports for the support of the Soviet Northern Fleet in the North Atlantic.

The plan would require these Soviet forces to punch through northern Finnish forces, cross Finnish territory, before attacking Norway's Finnmark region. Soviet divisions would also be directed against Sweden's northern Norrbotten county, pinning any Swedish forces there and protecting the main offensive's flank. Attacks into southern Finland would tie down Finnish forces, while Soviet units operating out of the Baltic states and Kalingrad would also make landings on the Swedish coast.

For NATO, the neutral Swedish air force was to play a key role in denying Soviet access across its air space and preventing Soviet anti-submarine aircraft crossing its territory to attack NATO targets in the North Atlantic. The Swedes were also secretly sharing intelligence information with NATO.

WAR IN THE NORTH

The forces of the Warsaw Pact launched their ground assault against the NATO forces in West Germany on 4 August 1985. However, the divisions of the Soviet 6th Combined Arms Army did not cross the Finnish and Norwegian borders until 7 August 1985. The Norwegians and Finns were on high alert due to the building international tension and the well-disguised, but not completely concealed, build-up of Soviet forces on their frontiers. The war in central Europe had the Nordic nations prepared for invasion at any moment.

In Norway's Finnmark region, border forces conducted a fighting withdrawal westwards, laying ambushes along the main routes of the Soviet advance. However, Soviet air assault helicopter-borne and naval landing forces struck airbases, ports, and other military installations ahead of the advancing 54th Motor Rifle Division.

To their south the Soviet 116th and 131st Motor Rifle Divisions advanced into Finland, across Lapland, with the 16th and 111th Motor Rifle Divisions following behind. Here they were heavily engaged by determined Finnish forces, even though the Leningrad Military District's 30th Guards Corps and elements of the 26th Corps had begun an attack into southern Finland when it became clear the Finns were not going to allow the Soviets free access across Lapland. Some in the Soviet command had thought the Finns might acquiesce to the Soviets' earlier request once actual military action was taken. They were badly mistaken.

As the Soviets advanced into Finland, they encountered Swedish air force units flying ground attack sorties against them in support of the Finns. The violation of Finnish neutrality, had drawn Sweden into the war against the Soviet Union.

By the end of the first week of the conflict in Scandinavia the Soviet 61st Independent Naval Landing Brigade had successfully taken Banak Air Station at the end of the Porsanger fjord in Norway after overcoming the battalion defending the airport. The 54th Motor Rifle Division, and the following 16th Motor Rifle Division, after it had cut through Finnish Lapland, had their advance slowed as they encountered the elite troops of Norway's Brigade Nord, which was being reinforced by brigades arriving from southern Norway. Meanwhile, Finnish resistance had stiffened along the rest of the front as their defence slowed the Soviet advance.

JUTLAND

Further south, Denmark's Jutland Division, alongside the West German 6. Panzergrenadierdivision, battled to defend Schlesweg-Holstein, protecting Danish Jutland and the north flank of Hamburg. While NATO and the Warsaw Pact struggled to assert their dominance over the western Baltic, the Warsaw Pact had yet to make any moves towards an amphibious assault on the Danish main island of Sjælland (Zealand) within the first week of the war.

NORTHERN SCANDINAVIA

The second week of the conflict in Norway had seen the arrival of NATO reinforcements in the form of the British/Netherlands Commando Brigade, which came ashore at Trondheim. However, the US 2nd Marine Division was still being held back for their possible use in Denmark if required. The Soviet air force had concentrated on targeting Norway's airports and seaports with bombing, though had had to run the gauntlet of NATO, Swedish, and Finnish fighter interception.

More Norwegian brigades had also begun to arrive in Finnmark, though

the rapid advance of the Soviet forces had seen the focus of the Norwegian defence concentrated around the mountain passes in the west of Finnmark.

In the meantime, the Finns and Swedes had formed a rough defensive line running along the Finno-Swedish border in the west, and from Äkäslompolo to Salla in Finnish Lapland, effectively forming a southern barrier along the path of the Soviet advance. The Soviets seemed content not to press too hard southwards, having achieved their passage into Norway.

The Soviet attack into southern Finland had pushed past Lappeenranta towards Kouvola, while the attack out of Karelia had lost momentum before reaching Joensuu, becoming bogged down in heavy fighting among the forests and lakes.

DENMARK

By the beginning of the second week, despite a determined defence, the Danish Jutland Division and the West German 6. *Panzergrenadierdivision* had been pushed north beyond Kiel and Schleswig, and faced determined attacks from Polish and Soviet divisions as they withdrew across the Danish border on 13 August 1985. They eventually established a defensive line south of Haderslev.

Two days later the US 2nd Marine Division was committed to the battle for Jutland when they landed on the west coast of the peninsula, coinciding with the main NATO counterattack towards Bremen and Hamburg from the south.

The Jutland Division began to push south parallel to the US Marines. By end of the first day of the offensive they had retaken the city of Schleswig and had begun to move towards Rendsburg and the Nord-Ostsee Kanal connecting the North Sea and the Baltic Sea (see map on page 85).

THE WAR GOES ON

As the third week of the war began the situation across the Nordic front was poised precariously. In Norway, the Norwegians and their NATO allies held the passes that led to central Norway, while Swedes and Finns held the Soviets in Northern Lapland and in Finland's southeast. However, the Warsaw Pact had yet to commit any of their Baltic amphibious landing forces to battle, with the possibility of landings in the Denmark islands, Swedish Gotland or the mainland coast, or even in southern Finland. The Soviets continued to mobilise reserve units from across the Soviet Union, any of which could be committed to Nordic or Central European fronts.

FORCES IN WORLD WAR III

Finland gained its independence after the 1917 Russian Revolution, only to have it threatened again in 1939 by Soviet invasion. The people of Finland rallied and fought a tenacious and savage defence of their homeland during the Winter War, the outcome of which saw Finland retain its independence. Unfortunately the neighbouring Baltic states of Estonia, Latvia, and Lithuania found themselves once more under the Russian boot following a brief period of independence.

The Finns joined Germany's war against the Soviet Union in 1941 with the aim of gaining territory lost in 1939, pushing past their old frontiers, but frustrated their German allies by not pushing beyond Leningrad and further into the Soviet Union. Eventually as the tide of World War II turned against Germany, they found themselves once more under Soviet attack in the summer of 1944. They fought the Soviets to a standstill and were able to retain their independence.

Under their peace terms with the Soviets, they were forced to turn on the Germans operating in the north of Finland and push them back across the Norwegian border.

At the end of World War II, Finland was forced to abide by a number of military restrictions and concessions by the 1947 Treaty of Paris. Finland was restored to its borders of 1 January 1941 (thus confirming its territorial losses after the Winter War of 1939-40), except for the former province of Petsamo (Pechenga), which was ceded to the Soviet Union.

COLD WAR

The Finnish military and political situation was difficult and complex during the Cold War because of the country's close proximity to the Soviet Union. A Friendship, Cooperation and Mutual Assistance Pact signed in 1948 gave the Soviet Union influence on Finnish foreign policy. Finland was to provide guarantees that it would not allow its territory to be used for an attack against the Soviet Union. The treaty also led to a tendency within Finland to avoid statements and acts that could be considered anti-Soviet. The media was self-censored, anti-Soviet books were removed from libraries, and the authorities had the power to censor movies. However, Finland remained a Western market economy, while also benefitting from preferential trade with the Soviet Union. Military arms purchases were balanced between East and West as part of the effort not to show particular favouritism.

The Soviet Union also recognised Finland's position of neutrality. As a neutral Nordic state Finland's foreign policy endeavoured to stay outside the conflicts of interest between the great powers and military alliances. They maintained friendly relations with their neighbours as well as all other States, and contributed to the security of Europe.

During the Cold War most of the main western powers were surprisingly willing and ready to support Finland, without definite military undertakings. Possible military support would be given on an ad hoc basis in a war situation and only if Finland chose the West rather than the Soviets. An attack by the West simply was not considered a very serious option. Real contingency plans were aimed at fighting potential Soviet ground forces attacks. For security reasons, these were not put on paper, but rather entrusted to selected key military personnel responsible for maintaining them. In 1974, newly appointed Chief of Defence General Lauri Sutela offered to present operational plans to his Supreme Commander, President Urho Kekkonen, but the latter respectfully declined, saying: "I'm not interested in details, but I rely on you and trust that you know what you have to do."

THE MILITARY AND EQUIPMENT

Finland introduced a Conscription Act in 1950 to provide a ready body of trained men to defend its territory if required. The basic term of duty would be 240 days, and for specialists and officers 330 days. In addition, 40 to 100 days participation in refresher training was compulsory.

By the 1980s, Finland had predominately training units rather then dedicated combat ready standing forces. However, if needed standing peacetime troops could be rapidly reinforced within hours from these reservists.

A fast deployment force of about 250,000 men, comprising the best-equipped Army brigades, the Frontier Guards, the Air Force and Navy could be made combat-ready through accelerated mobilisation within a few days.

The fully mobilised wartime Finnish Defence Force consisted of approximately 530,000 men drawn from a pool of one million trained reservists. Time permitting, mobilisation would be followed by a period of intense combat training. The bulk of these troops could be deployed within a week. Sparsely populated areas, such as Lapland, would receive reinforcements from central Finland.

TACTICS AND STRATEGIES

Finnish tactics and strategies were fundamentally defensive, with battle doctrine being modified in the decades between the 1950s and 1980s.

The Finns categorised their troops into local and general forces. The local forces are equipped mainly with light arms and mines. They formed a network covering the whole country, defended sensitive limited targets, and performed delaying actions in their local surroundings. They are also prepared to carry out mobile light infantry- and guerrilla-type operations.

The general forces of the Army were concentrated to defend, hold and reoccupy key areas. While the main function of the local forces was to slow down and wear out the enemy attack, while the primary task of the general forces was to repel the aggressor. This system of territorial defence was a flexible one, using mobility, battle endurance and exploitation of terrain to the fullest extent possible. Both types of forces provide support to each other in their respective primary tasks.

Throughout the 1960s and 1970s the Finns modernised their forces, replacing much of their World War II vintage equipment and weapons with new systems from both the West and Warsaw Pact. 50 T-54s were delivered between 1960 and 1961, and 70 T-55s were delivered between 1965 and 1967, all from the Soviet Union. 120 BTR-60s were delivered in 1976. They used British Comet tanks between 1960 and 1971, and Charioteer tanks between 1958 and 1979.

The 1980s saw the arrival of more modern vehicles including the BMP-1 infantry fighting vehicle and the T-72 main battle tank, as well as the home produced XA-180 Sisu Pasi 6-wheeled APC.

A variety of anti-tank guided missile systems were also purchased beginning with the French SS-11 and British Vickers Vigilant in the 1960s, before progressing to the US TOW and Soviet AT-4 Spigot and AT-5 Spandrel anti-tank systems in the early 1980s.

They developed their own 55mm recoilless anti-tank weapon in 1955, which like the similar looking but funtionally different Soviet RPG-7, was reloadable and fired a projectile with a shaped-charge HEAT round. These saw service well in to the 1980s and was further supplemented by US M72 LAW disposable anti-tank weapons as well as similar Swedish and French weapons.

FINLAND AND WORLD WAR III

The Soviet command had a number of wartime plans for Finland. Some involved the invasion and conquest of the whole of Finland, with Helsinki, Vaasa, and Oulu as the primary Soviet objectives and even involved the use of Finland as a launch point for the invasion of Sweden. Other plans varied between limited offensives, allowing Finland to maintain its neutrality, or requests for access to Finnish territory for troop movements.

However, the Soviet Union's main goal was the domination of the Norwegian Sea and Northern Norway to support the free passage of its Northern Fleet into the North Sea and the Atlantic Ocean. For this they initially demanded the Finns give them free passage across Lapland for Soviet northern forces attacking Norway. When the Finns refused, the Soviets instead attacked through Lapland towards Norway.

Other Soviet forces also attacked into southern Finland, tying down the bulk of the Finnish Defence Forces around their main population centres.

KAPTEENI HEIKKILÄ'S JÄÄKÄRI COMPANY

VAALIMAA BORDER
7 AUGUST 1985

VAALIMAA BORDER

Kapteeni (Captain) Matti Heikkilä looked through his binoculars across the field and the main road to Vaalimaantie that ran behind it. War in Europe had started a few days earlier, but so far all was quiet except for the intelligence reports coming to him from the forward scouts along the border.

His company was positioned on both sides of the road. Engineers had mined and boobytrapped the road as it entered the woods and ran to his lines. The Vaalimaa river bridge had also been prepared for demolition and the engineers were ready to blow it after the first few enemy vehicles had crossed it, isolating them from the rest of their column.

Heikkilä's orders were to slow down and disrupt the Soviet advance on this road. He had picked this spot as it gave his company a fighting chance to fall back once the enemy advance was halted, even if only momentarily.

On 7 August 1985 all hell broke loose. The forward scouts reported an armoured column crossing the border and advancing with speed up the road towards Hamina. Kapteeni Heikkilä quickly ordered his infantry and BMP-1 crews to prepare for combat. Also attached to his command was a platoon of T-72FM1 main battle tanks, positioned on his right flank.

The BMP-2 scouting elements and the first few T-72 tanks of the Soviets were let past the bridge before it was blown and they were cut off from their trailing elements. Anti-tank guided missiles and Finnish T-72FM1 tanks made short work of the isolated vehicles. However, while those were being handled, the Soviets had brought up an MTU-72 Armoured Bridge Layer to help the rest of the column cross the destroyed expanse of the bridge. It was time to fall back towards Virolahti.

VIROLAHTI

The company fell back in good order. Their new positions were in Virolahti, to the west of Virojoki. Time was of the essence here since it would not take long for the Soviets to span the gap in the bridge. The bridges leading to the centre of Virolahti were already destroyed leaving only the main road bridge intact, but prepared for demolition.

The main parts of Heikkilä's company took up positions on the perimeter of Virolahti, while the T-72FM1 platoon headed to the west side of Virolahti with one BMP-1 platoon.

It took only a few hours for the Soviets to approach Virolahti. They had changed their battle formation and this time advanced with a larger force of T-72 tanks in front with the infantry following behind mounted in BMP-2s.

The Soviet armour rushed across the bridge and made contact with the Finnish tanks and the BMP-1 platoon to the west, while the BMP-2 infantry started to attack the main positions of the company in Virolahti. One of the T-72FM1s and two BMP-1s were lost to the massed fire from the Soviet T-72s, forcing these Finnish platoons to fall back towards Hamina.

Meanwhile, the two remaining BMP-1 infantry platoons engaged the Soviet infantry. The exchange of fire saw the destruction of several BMP-2s, but the Finns lost two of their own BMP-1s in return.

Kapteeni Heikkilä's last act in Virolahti was to order the demolition of the last bridge before his force withdrew south.

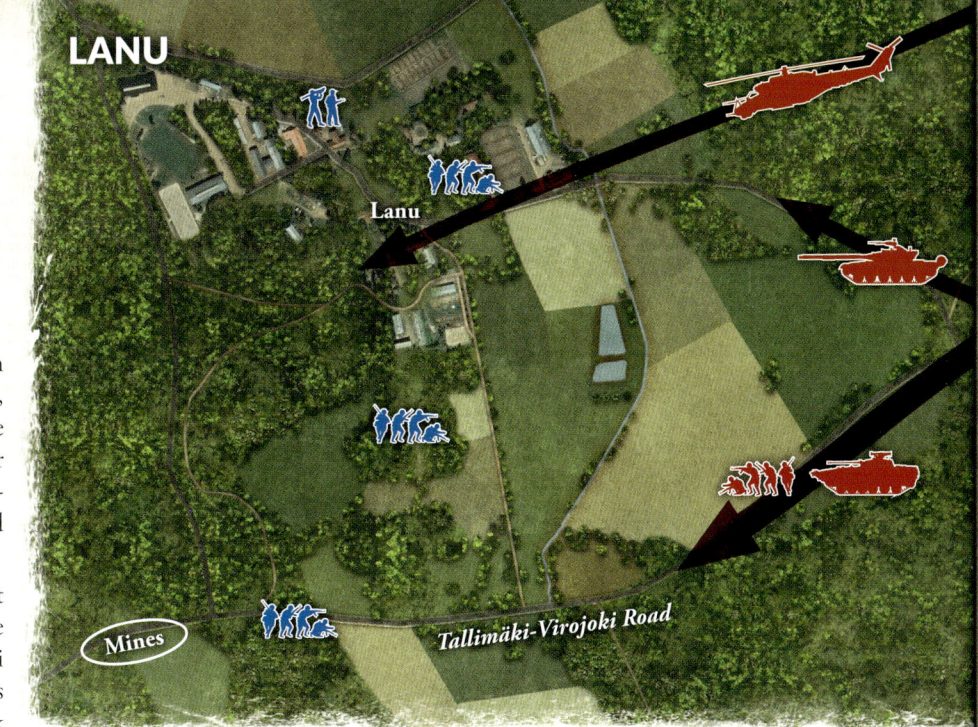

LANU

The retrograde movement from Virolahti was successfully executed, as most of the Soviet infantry were trapped behind the Virojoki River and the destroyed bridge. The company raced southwest and regrouped near Lanu.

Heikkilä's company took up yet another delaying position on the northwest side of Tallimäki-Virojoki Road in Lanu where the engineers had prepared another roadblock with mines and an abatis made up of felled trees before the Koulutilantie crossroads.

The following day the Soviets advanced more cautiously than on previous occasions when they emerged following the road from the east. The Soviet BMP-2s raced along the road west while their T-72s hung back in covering positions.

Heikkilä's ordered his company to open fire when the leading BMP-2s entered Ravijoki, managing to knock out a few of them before the Soviet infantry dismounted. The return fire from the overwatching Soviet T-72s was devastating. They took out several BMP-1s and forced one of the Finnish platoons to retreat back into better cover.

The Soviets then brought up their Mi-24 Hind attack helicopters. With little anti-air, except some ItO78s attached to the company, Kapteeni Heikkilä's company took heavy casualties. He ordered his company to fallback using the cover of the minor forest roads. The company had taken a beating, but performed well.

MÄNTLAHTI

The remainder of the company, now barely combat effective, withdrew to Mäntlahti. However, the timely arrival of reinforcements, a platoon of T-72FM1 tanks and T-55 Marksman anti-aircraft tanks, bolstered both the formation's strength and morale.

Kapteeni Heikkilä ordered one squad from his first platoon forward as scouts to the east side of Mäntlahti. They were to engage once they located the enemy, before hastily withdrawing, to "shoot and scoot" in other words.

The rest of the company took up positions inside of Mäntlahti ready to do something similar, while the T-72FM1 tanks and T-55 Marksman AA tanks stayed west of Mäntlahti. The T-72FM1s had orders to cover the withdrawal of Heikkilä's company.

The Soviets had a surprise up their sleeve. They had a company of BMP-2 infantry coming up from Kivisalmi Satama to the south where they had swum across the Kylänlahti Bay.

While the main force started their assault via the Tallimäki-Virojoki Road with T-72s and BMP-2 infantry, the lone company assaulted from the south, outflanking and overrunning Heikkilä's positions with ease.

The T-72FM1 tanks and T-55 Marksman AA tanks fell back west with one platoon of Heikkilä's infantry, while the remaining infantry were pushed north through the forest. Casualties had been light on both sides, but the surprise of the attack from the south had thrown the Finnish defensive plans into confusion.

Following this, Heikkilä's company was pulled out of the line to rearm and refit. The independence of Finland was under threat once more.

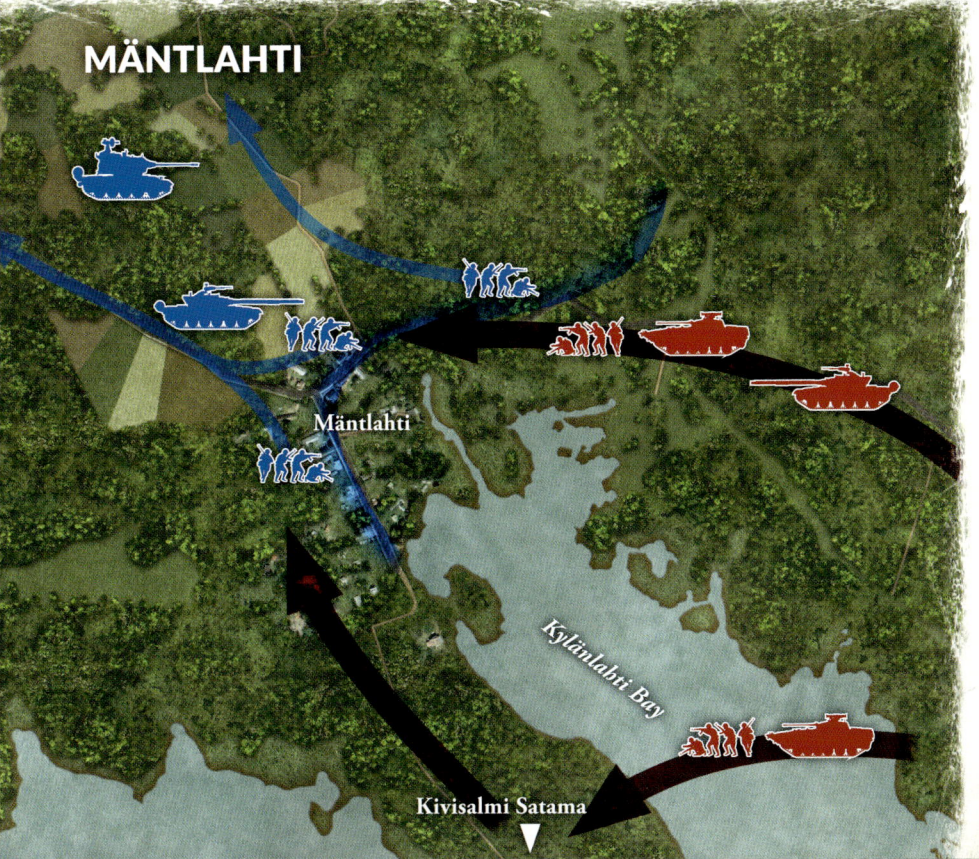

SUOMEN MAAVOIMAT
FINNISH FORCE

PANSSARIPRIKAATI

T-72FM1 ARMOURED COMPANY
TFI101 — 15

PANSSARIPRIKAATI

T-72FM2 ARMOURED COMPANY
TFI103 — 17

PANSSARIPRIKAATI

T-55M ARMOURED COMPANY
TFI105 — 19

PANSSARIPRIKAATI

BMP-1 JÄÄKÄRI COMPANY
TFI107 — 21

KARJALAN PRIKAATI

BTR-60 JÄÄKÄRI COMPANY
TFI110 — 25

ARTILLERY

2S1 CARNATION HOWITZER BATTERY
TFI113 — 27

120MM MORTAR PLATOON
TFI117 — 23

ARTILLERY

BM-21 HAIL ROCKET LAUNCHER BATTERY
TFI121 — 27

ANTI-AIRCRAFT

T-55 MARKSMAN ANTI-AIRCRAFT PLATOON
TFI115 — 28

ZSU-57-2 ANTI-AIRCRAFT PLATOON
TFI114 — 28

ANTI-AIRCRAFT

ITO 78 ANTI-AIRCRAFT MISSILE PLATOON
TFI130 — 29

OBSERVER

BMP-1 OP FORWARD OBSERVER
TFI122 — 27

AIRCRAFT

SWEDISH VIGGEN ATTACK GROUP
TSV118 — 53

RECONNAISSANCE

BMP-2 RECON PLATOON
TFI129 — 29

ANTI-TANK

PSTOHJ ANTI-TANK MISSILE PLATOON
TFI128 — 29

NATO ALLIED FORMATION

YOU MAY FIELD ONE NATO FORMATION AS AN ALLIED FORMATION

FORMATION SUPPORT
You may field compulsory Combat Units (with a black box) from the above Formations as Support Units.

FINNISH SPECIAL RULES

The Finnish Army has a number of features and weapons. These are reflected in the following special rules.

BAZOOKA SKIRTS

Finnish T-72FM1 and T-55M tanks did not have the BDD or ERA armour of the later model T-72 tanks used by the Soviets. To compensate for this, they are fitted with 'bazooka skirts', spaced armour to protect them from light, hand-held anti-tank weapons.

> Teams with Bazooka Skirts have a Side armour rating of 10 against HEAT weapons.

MANUAL TRACKING

Anti-aircraft weapons without modern radars or other electronic tracking systems have difficulty targetting fast-moving aircraft.

> Anti-aircraft Weapons with Manual Tracking add +1 to the score required To Hit Aircraft that are not Helicopters.

RADAR

Anti-aircraft radar on the T-55 Marksman makes tracking fast-moving aircraft much easier, especially at long range.

> The Twin 35mm L/90 gun on a T-55 Marksman has a Range of 40"/100cm against aircraft and does not suffer the usual +1 To Hit penalty for range over 16"/40cm when Shooting at Aircraft.

SWEDISH ALLIED SUPPORT

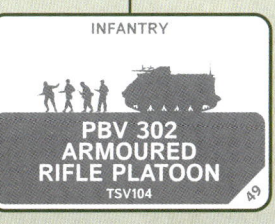

Rules for Swedish Formations and Units can be found on pages 40 to 53 of this book.

NATO ALLIED SUPPORT

Though Finland was officially neutral, their defensive posture was directed against the Soviet Union, though friendly relations were maintained. An outbeak of war between NATO and the Warsaw Pact would likely see Finland embroiled in some manner. Like Sweden, Finland was likely to lean towards fellow liberal democratic nations inside NATO for support.

You may take an NATO Allied Formation as part of your Force. A NATO Allied Formation can be from any other Force with a NATO Allied Formation in its support.

An Allied Formation obeys all the rules for its own nationality. An Allied Formation Commander can only join Units in its own Formation or nation, and only its Formation or national Units can benefit from its Command Leadership (see page 25 and 64 of *World War III: Team Yankee*).

An Allied Formation does not count as a Formation when determining if you have lost the game (see page 65 of *World War III: Team Yankee*).

T-72FM1 ARMOURED COMPANY

Vänrikki (second lieutenant) Joonas Mäkinen observed the road junction half a kilometre ahead of his platoon.

His platoon belonged to the 2nd Mechanised Brigade and they had been called up into service a few months earlier. They were all reservists, but had received a lot of additional training since their conscription service time had ended.

"I don't like this spot. Too much forest on both sides," he said to his crew. "Jaakko, do you see that opening on the left, 100 meters to our front left?" he asked of his driver.

"Yeah, I see it. Would give us way better position to fall back into cover," answered Korpraali (Corporal) Jaakko Lehtonen from his seat.

"Want me to drive us there?" he asked.

"Do it," Joonas replied.

Their T-72FM1 surged forward to get into the better position. "All Bertta, this is Bertta 1. We are moving up to a better position up ahead." Joonas radioed to the rest of his platoon.

"Contact, crossroads! T-72!" shouted the gunner Kersantti (Sergeant) Pekka Toivonen.

"Fire!" Jaakko shouted back.

"Firing!" came the reply. A fraction of a second later the emerging T-72 was engulfed in flames as the sabot round found its mark.

"All Bertta! Engage T-72s, crossroads!" Jaakko told the rest of the platoon. The platoon's two other T-72FM1s swung into action as their crews found spots to engage the following T-72s.

The narrow forest road and crossroad caused the following T-72s to bunch up and made them unable to bring all of their guns to bear. Soon three other enemy T-72s were destroyed and the crossroads was blocked by burning tanks.

"Disengage!" Jaakko told his platoon and one by one they slipped out of combat.

Finnish armoured forces were organised into an Armoured Brigade and two Reserve Armoured Brigades. The Armoured Brigade consisted of two armoured battalions and two armoured *Jääkäri* (jäger or light infantry) battalions, one mounted in BTR-60PB Soviet-built 8-wheeled APCs, the other in BMP infantry fighting vehicles.

The armoured battalions had begun rearming from T-55s to T-72M tanks from the mid-1980s. Each armoured battalion was organised into two companies of ten T-72 tanks each, and a company of infantry mounted in BMP-1 infantry fighting vehicles.

TANKS OF FINLAND

	T-72FM2	T-72FM1	T-55M
Front Armour:	17	15	13
Side Armour:	8	8	9
Weapon Range:	40"/100cm	40"/100cm	40"/100cm
Anti-tank:	22	22	19
Other:	ERA, Thermal Imaging, Brutal	Bazooka Skirts, Thermal Imaging, Brutal	Bazooka Skirts, Infra-red, Slow Firing

SUOMEN MAAVOIMAT
T-72FM1 ARMOURED COMPANY

You must field the Formation HQ and one Combat Unit from each black box.
You may also field one Combat Unit from each grey box.

T-72FM1 ARMOURED COMPANY HQ (TFI101)
1x T-72FM1 — **5 POINTS**

• Tank Formation • Bazooka Skirts • Thermal Imaging •

COURAGE 2+	SKILL 2+
MORALE 2+	ASSAULT 4+
REMOUNT 3+	COUNTERATTACK 3+

IS HIT ON 4+
FRONT 15 | SIDE 8 | TOP 2

TACTICAL	TERRAIN DASH	CROSS COUNTRY DASH	ROAD DASH	CROSS
10"/25cm	16"/40cm	24"/60cm	28"/70cm	3+

WEAPON	RANGE	ROF HALTED	ROF MOVING	ANTI-TANK	FIRE-POWER	NOTES
125mm 2A46 gun	40"/100cm	1	1	22	2+	Brutal, Laser Rangefinder, Stabiliser
12.7mm AA MG	20"/50cm	3	2	4	5+	
7.62mm MG	16"/40cm	1	1	2	6	

ARMOUR — T-72FM1 ARMOURED PLATOON (TFI102) — 15
ARMOUR — T-72FM1 ARMOURED PLATOON (TFI102) — 15
ARTILLERY — 2S1 CARNATION HOWITZER BATTERY (TFI113) — 27
ANTI-AIRCRAFT — ZSU-57-2 ANTI-AIRCRAFT PLATOON (TFI114) — 28

ARMOUR
- T-72FM1 ARMOURED PLATOON (TFI102) — 15
- T-72FM2 ARMOURED PLATOON (TFI104) — 17
- T-55M ARMOURED PLATOON (TFI106) — 19

INFANTRY
- BMP-1 JÄÄKÄRI PLATOON (TFI108) — 22
- BTR-60 JÄÄKÄRI PLATOON (TFI111) — 26

You may field a Combat Unit from a black box as a Support Unit for your Force.

SUOMEN MAAVOIMAT
T-72FM1 ARMOURED PLATOON

T-72FM1 ARMOURED PLATOON
3x T-72FM1 — **15 POINTS**

OPTIONS
- Fit up to one T-72FM1 tank with a Mine Clearing Device for +1 point.

The Finns purchased 65 T-72M1 from the Soviet Union in 1984. Soon after, they planned an upgrade program to their T-72 fleet. The first stage of this was the T-72FM1 (Finmod 1) which consisted of a new power plant that allowed faster turning and reverse, a new western Fire Control System, as well as new ammunition.

• Tank Unit • Bazooka Skirts • Thermal Imaging •

COURAGE 3+	SKILL 3+
MORALE 3+	ASSAULT 4+
REMOUNT 3+	COUNTERATTACK 4+

IS HIT ON 4+
FRONT 15 | SIDE 8 | TOP 2

TACTICAL	TERRAIN DASH	CROSS COUNTRY DASH	ROAD DASH	CROSS
10"/25cm	16"/40cm	24"/60cm	28"/70cm	3+

WEAPON	RANGE	ROF HALTED	ROF MOVING	ANTI-TANK	FIRE-POWER	NOTES
125mm 2A46 gun	40"/100cm	1	1	22	2+	Brutal, Laser Rangefinder, Stabiliser
12.7mm AA MG	20"/50cm	3	2	4	5+	
7.62mm MG	16"/40cm	1	1	2	6	

T-72FM2 ARMOURED COMPANY

The older T-72FM1 tanks from yliluutnantti (first lieutenant) Ilari Savolainen's company had been exchanged for the upgraded T-72FM2s a few weeks ago. Since then they had been training with their new equipment. Much on the new tank was familiar, the key differences were an improved engine, improved ammunition, and an overall new look with the tank's ERA blocks.

However, the time for training had ended. The company had been transported from their barracks by rail and unloaded from the train in Outokumpu, 50km east of Joensuu. The company was attached to a battlegroup that had been formed to counterattack the Soviet forces southeast of Joensuu. However, their first task was to eliminate the Soviet airborne landing at Joensuu Airfield.

"Celsius 1-0 to all Celsius, move out." Ilari radioed to the company and the attached infantry units.

Their mission was to attack the airfield from the northwest, pin the enemy in place while another pincer came from the southeast.

The Soviets had been able to land some transport aircraft after their initial landings were made by helicopter. The High Command expected there to be some light armour to resist the attacking Finns.

"Do we expect any heavier armour to be present?" asked Ilari's gunner.

"No, the heavier armour is still behind the Pielis River. I don't think the Soviets have the capability to airlift heavier tanks like T-80s," Ilari replied.

"Well, I think we will still get to try out our new ammo."

The company started to spread out to their predesigned positions on their map, with every vehicle commander given permission to find the best suitable spot.

Infantry units found their places amongst the T-72FM2s, ready to dash forward when the command was given.

"Alright, be prepared and find targets," Ilari told everyone.

"Got a target in the northeast corner of the hangar complex, silhouette matches BMD," came in from one of Ilari's platoons.

"Copy, take aim. We will hit them soon." Ilari replied.

As soon as the Finns got their first T-72 tanks they began planning improvements to them. The first wave has seen the addition of better ammunition and improved fire control systems, combining some the the latest western technology with tried and tested Soviet engineering. The next wave of modifications was the addition of explosive reactive armour (ERA) to improve the protection of the T-72s.

Some armoured companies have been equipped with these latest upgraded T-72FM2 tanks and can usually be found fighting alongside the newer B rmoured battalion organisation with two companies of ten T-72FM2 tanks each, but with a company of infantry mounted in BMP-2s instead of BMP-1s.

SUOMEN MAAVOIMAT
T-72FM2 ARMOURED COMPANY

You must field the Formation HQ and one Combat Unit from each black box.
You may also field one Combat Unit from each grey box.

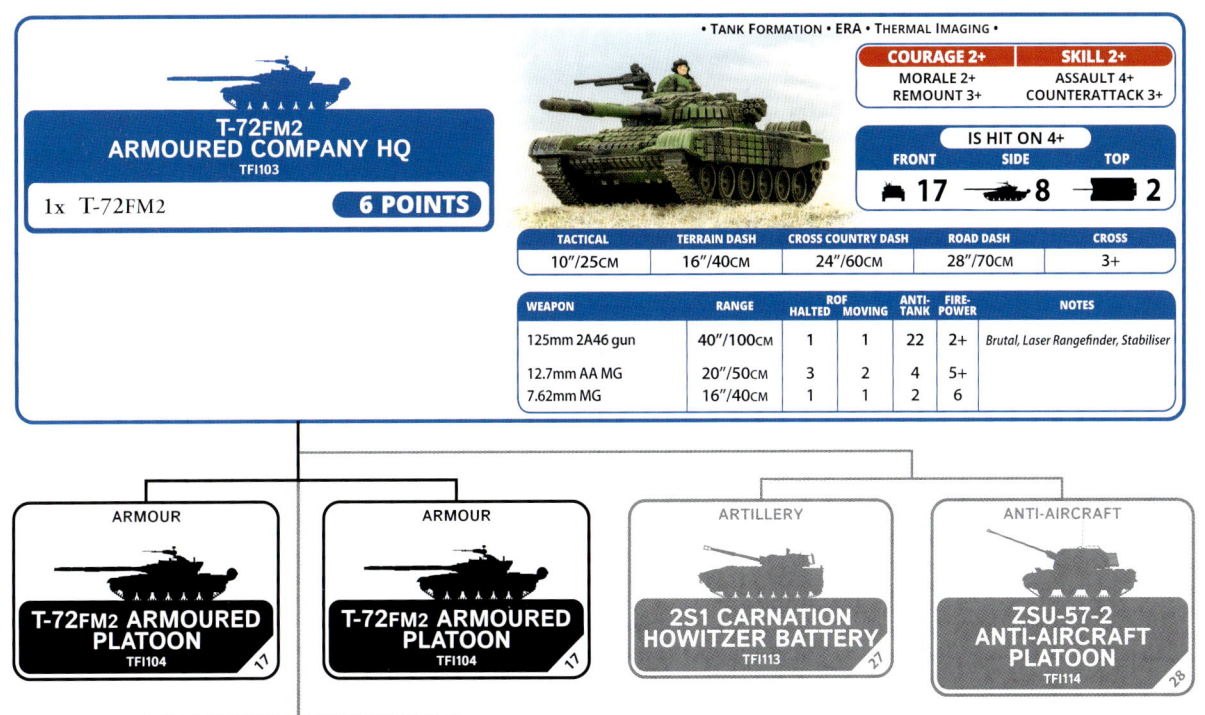

T-72FM2 ARMOURED COMPANY HQ — TFI103
1x T-72FM2 — **6 POINTS**

• Tank Formation • ERA • Thermal Imaging •

COURAGE 2+	SKILL 2+
MORALE 2+	ASSAULT 4+
REMOUNT 3+	COUNTERATTACK 3+

IS HIT ON 4+
FRONT	SIDE	TOP
17	8	2

TACTICAL	TERRAIN DASH	CROSS COUNTRY DASH	ROAD DASH	CROSS
10"/25cm	16"/40cm	24"/60cm	28"/70cm	3+

WEAPON	RANGE	ROF HALTED	ROF MOVING	ANTI-TANK	FIRE-POWER	NOTES
125mm 2A46 gun	40"/100cm	1	1	22	2+	Brutal, Laser Rangefinder, Stabiliser
12.7mm AA MG	20"/50cm	3	2	4	5+	
7.62mm MG	16"/40cm	1	1	2	6	

ARMOUR
- T-72FM2 ARMOURED PLATOON — TFI104 — 17

ARMOUR
- T-72FM2 ARMOURED PLATOON — TFI104 — 17

ARTILLERY
- 2S1 CARNATION HOWITZER BATTERY — TFI113 — 27

ANTI-AIRCRAFT
- ZSU-57-2 ANTI-AIRCRAFT PLATOON — TFI114 — 28

ARMOUR
- T-72FM1 ARMOURED PLATOON — TFI102 — 15
- T-72FM2 ARMOURED PLATOON — TFI104 — 17
- T-55M ARMOURED PLATOON — TFI106 — 19

INFANTRY
- BMP-2 JÄÄKÄRI PLATOON — TFI126 — 23
- BMP-1 JÄÄKÄRI PLATOON — TFI108 — 22
- BTR-60 JÄÄKÄRI PLATOON — TFI111 — 26

You may field a Combat Unit from a black box as a Support Unit for your Force.

SUOMEN MAAVOIMAT
T-72FM2 ARMOURED PLATOON

T-72FM2 ARMOURED PLATOON
3x T-72FM2 — **19 POINTS**

OPTIONS
- Fit up to one T-72FM2 tank with a Mine Clearing Device for +1 point.

The next step in the Finnish T-72 upgrade programme (FM2 or Finmod 2) added ERA armour (Kontakt-1) to the new engine, fire control system, and ammunition used with the T-72FM1 to create the T72FM2.

• Tank Unit • ERA • Thermal Imaging •

COURAGE 3+	SKILL 3+
MORALE 3+	ASSAULT 4+
REMOUNT 3+	COUNTERATTACK 4+

IS HIT ON 4+
FRONT	SIDE	TOP
17	8	2

TACTICAL	TERRAIN DASH	CROSS COUNTRY DASH	ROAD DASH	CROSS
10"/25cm	16"/40cm	24"/60cm	28"/70cm	3+

WEAPON	RANGE	ROF HALTED	ROF MOVING	ANTI-TANK	FIRE-POWER	NOTES
125mm 2A46 gun	40"/100cm	1	1	22	2+	Brutal, Laser Rangefinder, Stabiliser
12.7mm AA MG	20"/50cm	3	2	4	5+	
7.62mm MG	16"/40cm	1	1	2	6	

T-55M ARMOURED COMPANY

Even though the 100mm gun of the T-55 was an aging piece of technology in comparison to the T-72 tank's 125mm gun, it was decided improvements could be made and it was worth upgrading the Finnish T-55s to the new T-55M standard.

After the upgrades the T-55M was in fact better equipped than the standard T-72, except in the area of gun performance. It was still a capable platform to support infantry operations and the T-55Ms were given to three independent tank battalions. One of these battalions had been stationed northeast of Kajaani in the Paltamo-Hyrynsalmi-Suomussalmi area.

"So, we're to attack the flank of the advancing Soviet mechanised brigade which is pushing from Kostamus," Kapteeni (captain) Mika Jaakkola's battalion commander briefed the assembled company commanders.

"Aarne company will be with the 2nd Infantry Battalion and ambush the enemy between Heinälä and Iivantiira."

The briefing was short since time was of the essence and Mika Jaakkola's company quickly set about preparing their T-55Ms.

While the infantry engaged enemy infantry and IFVs, Jaakkola's T-55 company's task was to engage the enemy MBTs from the flanks. It was the best and only opportunity they had against the newer T-72 and T-80 MBTs.

"Hey Mika, at least we can do something to those newer Soviet tanks, just don't get caught by the return fire," grinned one of Mika's platoon leaders.

"Hah! They won't even have time to see us before we're gone," Mika replied.

When he returned to his command tank he asked if everything was ready.

"Yeah she purrs like a kitten now," Mika's driver answered.

"Kitten with sharpened claws," his loader grinned before disappearing into the turret.

"Good. Let's go give our 'friends' some surprise welcoming presents," Mika laughed back at them and climbed to his own position. The V-12 engines of the company let out roars of approval as they came to life.

"Aarne company will follow the 2nd Infantry Battalion, 1st Platoon with 2nd Infantry Company, and 2nd Platoon with the 3rd Infantry. 3rd Platoon will be with the 1st Infantry, as will I," Jaakkola informed the rest of the company.

"Name of the game is fire and manoeuvre. Be quick and stealthy if you can. Good luck gents," Mika ended.

The Finnish army ordered their first 50 T-54 tanks from the Soviet Union in 1960 to be delivered the following year. They ordered 70 of the improved model, the T-55, in 1965 which had been all delivered by 1967. In the 1980s the Finns began upgrading their 70 T-55 tanks to T-55M standard. The upgrade consisted of an improved Swedish Bofors fire control system, Belgian Mecar armour piercing fin-stablised discarding sabot ammunition (APFSDS), a 71mm Bofors Lyran illumination grenade mortar, and eight 76mm Wegmann smoke grenade dischargers. A thermal sleeve was added around the gun barrel to improve accuracy. In addition to the illumination grenades, night fighting capabilities were further enhanced with an Infra-Red (IR) searchlight. Protection and self-defence were improved with new side skirts and a 12.7mm machine-gun for the loader. Additional armour was tested, but not included in the final upgrade.

The two Reserve Armoured Brigades each had two Armoured Battalions equipped with T-55 tanks and a *Jääkäri* Battalion in BTR-60s. Each reserve armoured battalion was organised with two companies of ten T-55M tanks each, and a company of infantry mounted in BMP-1 infantry fighting vehicles.

SUOMEN MAAVOIMAT
T-55M ARMOURED COMPANY

You must field the Formation HQ and one Combat Unit from each black box.
You may also field one Combat Unit from each grey box.

T-55M ARMOURED COMPANY HQ
TFI105

1x T-55M — **2 POINTS**

• TANK FORMATION • BAZOOKA SKIRTS • INFRA-RED (IR) •

COURAGE 2+ — MORALE 2+, REMOUNT 3+
SKILL 2+ — ASSAULT 4+, COUNTERATTACK 3+

IS HIT ON 4+ — FRONT 13, SIDE 9, TOP 2

TACTICAL	TERRAIN DASH	CROSS COUNTRY DASH	ROAD DASH	CROSS
10"/25CM	14"/35CM	20"/50CM	24"/60CM	4+

WEAPON	RANGE	ROF HALTED	ROF MOVING	ANTI-TANK	FIRE-POWER	NOTES
100mm D10-T gun	40"/100CM	1	1	19	2+	Laser Rangefinder, Slow Firing
12.7mm AA MG	20"/50CM	3	2	4	5+	
7.62mm MG	16"/40CM	1	1	2	6	

ARMOUR — T-55M ARMOURED PLATOON — TFI106 (19)
ARMOUR — T-55M ARMOURED PLATOON — TFI106 (19)
ARTILLERY — 2S1 CARNATION HOWITZER BATTERY — TFI113 (27)
ANTI-AIRCRAFT — ZSU-57-2 ANTI-AIRCRAFT PLATOON — TFI114 (28)

ARMOUR
- T-72FM1 ARMOURED PLATOON — TFI102 (15)
- T-72FM2 ARMOURED PLATOON — TFI104 (17)
- T-55M ARMOURED PLATOON — TFI106 (19)

INFANTRY
- BMP-1 JÄÄKÄRI PLATOON — TFI108 (22)
- BTR-60 JÄÄKÄRI PLATOON — TFI111 (26)

You may field a Combat Unit from a black box as a Support Unit for your Force.

SUOMEN MAAVOIMAT
T-55M ARMOURED PLATOON

T-55M ARMOURED PLATOON
3x T-55M — **7 POINTS**

OPTIONS
- Fit up to one T-55M tank with a Mine Clearing Device for +1 point.

• TANK UNIT • BAZOOKA SKIRTS • INFRA-RED (IR) •

COURAGE 3+ — MORALE 3+, REMOUNT 3+
SKILL 3+ — ASSAULT 4+, COUNTERATTACK 4+

IS HIT ON 4+ — FRONT 13, SIDE 9, TOP 2

TACTICAL	TERRAIN DASH	CROSS COUNTRY DASH	ROAD DASH	CROSS
10"/25CM	14"/35CM	20"/50CM	24"/60CM	4+

WEAPON	RANGE	ROF HALTED	ROF MOVING	ANTI-TANK	FIRE-POWER	NOTES
100mm D10-T gun	40"/100CM	1	1	19	2+	Laser Rangefinder, Slow Firing
12.7mm AA MG	20"/50CM	3	2	4	5+	
7.62mm MG	16"/40CM	1	1	2	6	

With the arrival of the T-72 tanks, the T-55 tanks were relegated to the Reserve Armoured brigades. However, after the T-55 tanks' extensive upgrade to the T-55M, many considered it a superior tank to the unmodified T-72Ms as they arrived from the Soviet Union, with the T-55M crews out-shooting the T-72s in early exercises.

ARMOURED JÄÄKÄRI COMPANY

"All platoons are ready for the counterassault, BMPs report full readiness," Luutnantti Viljo Mäki reported to his company commander Kapteeni Riku Rantala.

Rantala's BMP Jääkäri Company was one of three tasked to this counterassault into Helsinki-Vantaa Airport where a strong Soviet Air Landing Battalion had inserted and had taken possession of the facilities.

"Good. Let's go over the plan one more time. Fast movement, fire on the move if you have to. First and third platoons at the front maintaining a wide spread. Second platoon to remain as overwatch fire support with priority to take out any spotted armour with their missiles.

"We will be rolling over open ground to reach the hangars, regardless of the circumstances do not stop. Once at the hangars, dismount and start pushing into the buildings. When the first building is secured second platoon will follow up and join the attack," Rantala ended the quick recap of the plan.

Acknowledgments from all of the platoons were short. This was something that they had been trained for many times over and done refresher exercises over the years.

Rantala switched to the battalion level radio and listened while some final commands were transmitted to the different units participating to this assault. A company of the new T-72FM2 tanks were also tasked to this assault.

Indirect fire support was to be given by each company's own mortar platoon, but just in case, there was a full battery of 2s1 Carnation self-propelled howitzers and even a rocket launcher battery if things went south.

The Carnations were also tasked with laying down covering smoke to help conceal the attacking BMPs and T-72FM2s from the enemy.

Finally, the word came over the comms channel from the task force commander, "Moukari 15, Leka 01, suppressive fire and smoke in ten seconds. All Leka will move out in 1 minute." Rantala passed on the orders to all of his platoons and the engines of BMPs were started all around him.

The final seconds passed by and the artillery opened fire. "Good luck gentlemen, Iske ja Murra!*" Rantala wished to all of his platoons. "Leka 01, Leka 20 moving," he informed the task force commander.

*Armoured Brigade's motto, roughy translates to "Hit and Break."

In the 1980s the Finnish armoured brigades underwent organisational changes as Finland purchased more vehicles and equipment. One major change was to convert their armoured brigades to mixed formations with two armoured companies of tanks and one company of armoured infantry in BMPs.

The final organisation of the BMP mounted *Jääkärikomppania* (light infantry or jäger company) in the armoured battalions consisted of three armoured infantry platoons and an 81mm mortar platoon.

FINNISH BMPS

BMP-1
Front Armour: 2
Gun Range: 16"/40cm
Anti-tank: 12
Other: HEAT
Slow Firing

BMP-1 (WITH PSTOHJ 82)
Front Armour: 2
Gun Range: 16"/40cm
Anti-tank: 12
Other: HEAT
Slow Firing
Missile Range: 40"/100cm
Anti-tank: 19

BMP-2
Front Armour: 2
Gun Range: 20"/50cm
Anti-tank: 10
Other: Anti-helicopter
Stabiliser
Missile Range: 48"/120cm
Anti-tank: 21

SUOMEN MAAVOIMAT
BMP-1 JÄÄKÄRI COMPANY

You must field the Formation HQ and one Combat Unit from each black box.
You may also field one Combat Unit from each grey box.

BMP-1 JÄÄKÄRI COMPANY HQ
TFI107

1x RK 62 team
1x BMP-1 (TFI109)

1 POINT

OPTIONS
- Arm BMP-1 transport with PstOhj 82 (AT-4) missile for +1 point.

• INFANTRY FORMATION • HQ TRANSPORT •

COURAGE 2+	SKILL 2+
MORALE 2+	ASSAULT 4+
RALLY 2+	COUNTERATTACK 3+

IS HIT ON	INFANTRY SAVE
4+	3+

TACTICAL	TERRAIN DASH	CROSS COUNTRY DASH	ROAD DASH	CROSS
8"/20CM	8"/20CM	12"/30CM	12"/30CM	AUTO

WEAPON	RANGE	ROF HALTED	ROF MOVING	ANTI-TANK	FIRE-POWER	NOTES
RK 62 assault rifle team	8"/20CM	3	3	1	6	Pinned ROF 1

INFANTRY

BMP-1 JÄÄKÄRI PLATOON
TFI108 — 22

INFANTRY

BMP-1 JÄÄKÄRI PLATOON
TFI108 — 22

BMP-2 JÄÄKÄRI PLATOON
TFI126 — 23

ANTI-TANK

95 S 58-61 ANTI-TANK PLATOON
TFI119 — 26

ARTILLERY

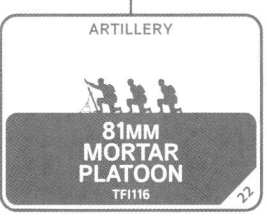

81MM MORTAR PLATOON
TFI116 — 22

INFANTRY

BMP-1 JÄÄKÄRI PLATOON
TFI108 — 22

ARMOUR

T-72FM1 ARMOURED PLATOON
TFI102 — 15

T-72FM2 ARMOURED PLATOON
TFI104 — 17

T-55M ARMOURED PLATOON
TFI106 — 19

ANTI-AIRCRAFT

ITO 78 ANTI-AIRCRAFT MISSILE PLATOON
TFI130 — 29

ARTILLERY

120MM MORTAR PLATOON
TFI117 — 23

You may field a Combat Unit from a black box as a Support Unit for your Force.

SUOMEN MAAVOIMAT
BMP-1 JÄÄKÄRI PLATOON

BMP-1 JÄÄKÄRI PLATOON
- 6x KK PKM MG team with 66 KES 75 anti-tank
- 3x BMP-1 (TFI109) — **6 POINTS**

- 4x KK PKM MG team with 66 KES 75 anti-tank
- 2x BMP-1 (TFI109) — **4 POINTS**

OPTIONS
- Replace one KK PKM MG team with an APILAS anti-tank team for +1 point.
- Arm all BMP-1 transports with PstOhj 82 (AT-4) missiles for +1 point for the Unit.

• INFANTRY UNIT •

COURAGE 3+	SKILL 3+
MORALE 3+	ASSAULT 4+
RALLY 3+	COUNTERATTACK 4+

IS HIT ON	INFANTRY SAVE
4+	3+

TACTICAL	TERRAIN DASH	CROSS COUNTRY DASH	ROAD DASH	CROSS
8"/20CM	8"/20CM	12"/30CM	12"/30CM	AUTO

WEAPON	RANGE	ROF HALTED	ROF MOVING	ANTI-TANK	FIRE-POWER	NOTES
KK PKM MG team	16"/40CM	3	2	2	6	
or 66 KES 75 anti-tank	12"/30CM	1	1	12	5+	HEAT, Slow Firing
OPTIONAL APILAS anti-tank team	16"/40CM	1	1	21	3+	Assault 5, HEAT, Slow Firing

The firepower of the armoured *Jääkärijoukkue* (Jäger platoon) comes from their three 7.62mm KK PKM general purpose machine-guns, backed up by the *Jääkäri*'s individual weapons, the 7.62mm RK 62 (a licenced copy of the AK-47) and the APILAS anti-tank rocket. For close range anti-tank self-defence they are also armed with disposable 66 KES 75 (M72 LAW) anti-tank weapons.

SUOMEN MAAVOIMAT
BMP-1 TRANSPORT

• TANK ATTACHMENT • AMPHIBIOUS • INFRA-RED (IR) • PASSENGERS 2 •

COURAGE 3+	SKILL 3+
MORALE 3+	ASSAULT 5+
REMOUNT 3+	COUNTERATTACK 5+

IS HIT ON 4+		
FRONT	SIDE	TOP
2	2	1

TACTICAL	TERRAIN DASH	CROSS COUNTRY DASH	ROAD DASH	CROSS
10"/25CM	16"/40CM	28"/70CM	32"/80CM	3+

WEAPON	RANGE	ROF HALTED	ROF MOVING	ANTI-TANK	FIRE-POWER	NOTES
73mm 2A28 gun	16"/40CM	1	1	12	3+	HEAT, Slow Firing
7.62mm MG	16"/40CM	3	3	2	6	
OPTIONAL PstOhj 82 (AT-4) missile	8"/20CM–40"/100CM	1	-	19	3+	Guided, HEAT

SUOMEN MAAVOIMAT
81MM MORTAR PLATOON

81MM MORTAR PLATOON
- 3x 81 KRH 71 mortar
- 3x BTR-60 (TFI112) — **3 POINTS**

- 2x 81 KRH 71 mortar
- 2x BTR-60 (TFI112) — **2 POINTS**

81mm *Kranaatinheitinjoukkue*, or Grenade Launcher Platoon, medium mortars provide short to medium fire support at short notice, bringing high-explosive and smoke on targets quickly and effectively.

• INFANTRY UNIT • HEAVY WEAPON •

COURAGE 3+	SKILL 3+
MORALE 3+	ASSAULT 6
RALLY 3+	COUNTERATTACK 4+

IS HIT ON	INFANTRY SAVE
4+	3+

TACTICAL	TERRAIN DASH	CROSS COUNTRY DASH	ROAD DASH	CROSS
8"/20CM	8"/20CM	12"/30CM	12"/30CM	AUTO

WEAPON	RANGE	ROF HALTED	ROF MOVING	ANTI-TANK	FIRE-POWER	NOTES
81 KRH 71 mortar	56"/140CM	ARTILLERY		1	4+	Smoke Bombardment

SUOMEN MAAVOIMAT
BMP-2 JÄÄKÄRI PLATOON

BMP-2 JÄÄKÄRI PLATOON
- 6x KK PKM MG team with 66 KES 75 anti-tank
- 3x BMP-2 (TFI127) — **8 POINTS**

- 4x KK PKM MG team with 66 KES 75 anti-tank
- 2x BMP-2 (TFI127) — **5 POINTS**

OPTIONS
- Replace one KK PKM MG team with an APILAS anti-tank team for +1 point.

Finland bought both BMP-1s and BMP-2s in significant numbers, these being the most advanced and modern vehicles available to transport and support the *panssarijääkärit* (armoured riflemen) in battle. Usually the infantry units ride in the BMP-1, which due to its smaller turret fitted a full squad of eight in the rear compartment, while the recon infantry and anti-tank units rode in the BMP-2, which only allowed for six passengers.

• INFANTRY UNIT •

COURAGE 3+	SKILL 3+
MORALE 3+	ASSAULT 4+
RALLY 3+	COUNTERATTACK 4+

IS HIT ON	INFANTRY SAVE
4+	3+

TACTICAL	TERRAIN DASH	CROSS COUNTRY DASH	ROAD DASH	CROSS
8"/20CM	8"/20CM	12"/30CM	12"/30CM	AUTO

WEAPON	RANGE	HALTED	MOVING	ANTI-TANK	FIRE-POWER	NOTES
KK PKM MG team	16"/40CM	3	2	2	6	
or 66 KES 75 anti-tank	12"/30CM	1	1	12	5+	HEAT, Slow Firing
OPTIONAL APILAS anti-tank team	16"/40CM	1	1	21	3+	Assault 5, HEAT, Slow Firing

SUOMEN MAAVOIMAT
BMP-2 TRANSPORT

• TANK ATTACHMENT • AMPHIBIOUS • INFRA-RED (IR) • PASSENGERS 2 •

COURAGE 3+	SKILL 3+
MORALE 3+	ASSAULT 5+
REMOUNT 3+	COUNTERATTACK 5+

IS HIT ON 4+		
FRONT	SIDE	TOP
2	2	1

TACTICAL	TERRAIN DASH	CROSS COUNTRY DASH	ROAD DASH	CROSS
10"/25CM	16"/40CM	24"/60CM	32"/80CM	3+

WEAPON	RANGE	HALTED	MOVING	ANTI-TANK	FIRE-POWER	NOTES
30mm 2A42 gun	20"/50CM	3	2	10	5+	Anti-helicopter, Stabiliser
7.62mm MG	16"/40CM	3	3	2	6	
PstOhj 82M (AT-5) missile	8"/20CM–48"/120CM	1	-	21	3+	Guided, HEAT

SUOMEN MAAVOIMAT
120MM MORTAR PLATOON

120MM MORTAR PLATOON
- 3x 120 KRH 73 mortar
- 3x BTR-60 (TFI112) — **4 POINTS**

- 2x 120 KRH 73 mortar
- 2x BTR-60 (TFI112) — **3 POINTS**

For heavier supporting fire the Finnish infantry call on the 120mm KRH heavy mortars to provide high-explosive and smoke.

• INFANTRY UNIT • HEAVY WEAPON •

COURAGE 3+	SKILL 3+
MORALE 3+	ASSAULT 6
RALLY 3+	COUNTERATTACK 4+

IS HIT ON	INFANTRY SAVE
4+	3+

TACTICAL	TERRAIN DASH	CROSS COUNTRY DASH	ROAD DASH	CROSS
4"/10CM	4"/10CM	6"/15CM	8"/20CM	3+

WEAPON	RANGE	HALTED	MOVING	ANTI-TANK	FIRE-POWER	NOTES
120 KRH 73 mortar	56"/140CM	ARTILLERY		3	3+	Smoke Bombardment

JÄÄKÄRI COMPANY

By the 1980s the BTR-60 was no longer well suited for assault operations. However, it was a good fire support vehicle against lightly armoured targets like BMPs and other BTR-60s or to pin down advancing infantry.

Yliluutnantti Vesa Vierikko's company had taken up delaying positions near a critical road junction. Their mission was to cause damage to the attacking Soviet forces and then fall back to their next positions. Most of the work would be done by the minefields and the roadblock that had been setup by the pioneers a day before. The plan also relied on the mortar platoon being able to fire rapidly into the dismounting Soviet forces once the battle had begun.

Vierikko's company had deployed on both sides of the road with most of the company's APILAS anti-tank launchers set up on one side with excellent side shot opportunities once the first vehicle was immobilised by the anti-tank mines.

The sound of engines in the distance revealed that the Soviets were coming. It would not be long until they could spring their surprise on the enemy. Vierikko's men would make them pay dearly, as their fathers and grandfathers had done years before.

"Jaakko, have the mortars ready to fire, first target Taneli 1," Vierikko told his forward observer.

The first vehicles, BMP-2 IFVs, rolled into view unaware of the coming ambush about to be sprung by their Finnish adversaries.

When the first BMP-2 hit the mines on the road the APILAS teams were already firing on the trailing vehicles. In quick succession the first three BMP-2s were immobilised or destroyed. Their infantry attempted to dismount their vehicles, only to be hit by the Finnish mortars who had already sent their regards into the air.

The remaining Soviet BMP-2s quickly opened up and started to suppress the Finnish positions, while their riflemen occupants dismounted and returned fire. Another round from the APILAS tank-hunters silenced yet another BMP-2.

"Jaakko, Tali 2. After that the whole Mekka," Vierikko directed his forward observer.

Mortar rounds kept on coming and then the big salvo hit the ground behind the Soviets.

"Break off!" Vierikko shouted to his men.

The order was passed around, squad by squad, and then platoon by platoon the Finns began to break off from contact.

One armoured Jäger (*Jääkäri*) battalion in each armoured brigade was mounted in BTR-60 8-wheeled armoured personnel carriers, while the *Jääkäri* Brigades in the south of Finland also had one of their four battalions mounted in BTR-60 APCs.

Each battalion is organised into three jäger companies, with three *Jääkäri* platoons and a recoilless rifle platoon armed with 95 S 58-61 anti-tank recoilless rifles, as well as 81mm and 120mm mortar platoons.

SUOMEN MAAVOIMAT
BTR-60 JÄÄKÄRI COMPANY

You must field the Formation HQ and one Combat Unit from each black box.
You may also field one Combat Unit from each grey box.

BTR-60 JÄÄKÄRI COMPANY HQ
TFI110

1x RK 62 team
1x BTR-60 (TFI112)

1 POINT

• INFANTRY FORMATION • HQ TRANSPORT •

COURAGE 2+	SKILL 2+
MORALE 2+	ASSAULT 4+
RALLY 2+	COUNTERATTACK 3+

IS HIT ON	INFANTRY SAVE
4+	3+

TACTICAL	TERRAIN DASH	CROSS COUNTRY DASH	ROAD DASH	CROSS
8"/20CM	8"/20CM	12"/30CM	12"/30CM	AUTO

WEAPON	RANGE	ROF HALTED	ROF MOVING	ANTI-TANK	FIRE-POWER	NOTES
RK 62 assault rifle team	8"/20CM	3	3	1	6	Pinned ROF 1

INFANTRY

BTR-60 JÄÄKÄRI PLATOON
TFI111 — 26

INFANTRY
BTR-60 JÄÄKÄRI PLATOON
TFI111 — 26

ANTI-TANK

95 S 58-61 ANTI-TANK PLATOON
TFI119 — 26

ARTILLERY
81MM MORTAR PLATOON
TFI116 — 22

INFANTRY
BTR-60 JÄÄKÄRI PLATOON
TFI111 — 26

ARMOUR

T-72FM1 ARMOURED PLATOON
TFI102 — 15

T-72FM2 ARMOURED PLATOON
TFI104 — 17

T-55M ARMOURED PLATOON
TFI106 — 19

ANTI-AIRCRAFT

ITO 78 ANTI-AIRCRAFT MISSILE PLATOON
TFI130 — 29

ARTILLERY

120MM MORTAR PLATOON
TFI117 — 23

You may field a Combat Unit from a black box as a Support Unit for your Force.

SUOMEN MAAVOIMAT
BTR-60 JÄÄKÄRI PLATOON

BTR-60 JÄÄKÄRI PLATOON
- 7x KK 62 MG team with 66 KES 75 anti-tank
- 2x 55 S 55 anti-tank team
- 4x BTR-60 (TFI112) — **8 POINTS**

- 5x KK 62 MG team with 66 KES 75 anti-tank
- 1x 55 S 55 anti-tank team
- 3x BTR-60 (TFI112) — **5 POINTS**

OPTIONS
- Replace all 55 S 55 anti-tank teams with APILAS anti-tank teams for +1 point each.

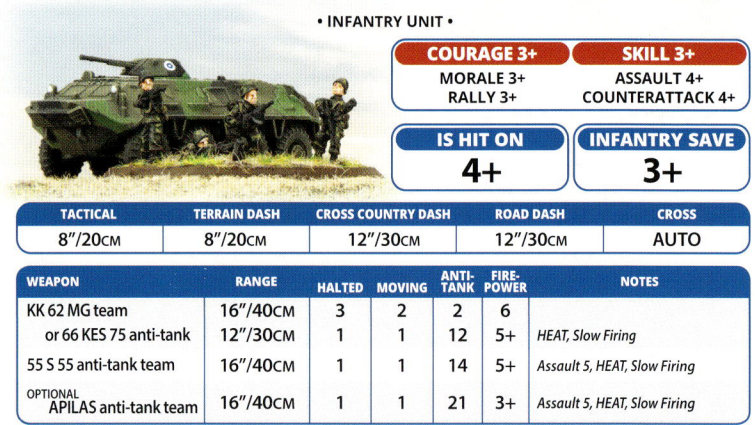

• INFANTRY UNIT •

COURAGE 3+	SKILL 3+
MORALE 3+ RALLY 3+	ASSAULT 4+ COUNTERATTACK 4+

IS HIT ON	INFANTRY SAVE
4+	3+

TACTICAL	TERRAIN DASH	CROSS COUNTRY DASH	ROAD DASH	CROSS
8"/20CM	8"/20CM	12"/30CM	12"/30CM	AUTO

WEAPON	RANGE	HALTED	MOVING	ANTI-TANK	FIRE-POWER	NOTES
KK 62 MG team	16"/40CM	3	2	2	6	
or 66 KES 75 anti-tank	12"/30CM	1	1	12	5+	HEAT, Slow Firing
55 S 55 anti-tank team	16"/40CM	1	1	14	5+	Assault 5, HEAT, Slow Firing
OPTIONAL APILAS anti-tank team	16"/40CM	1	1	21	3+	Assault 5, HEAT, Slow Firing

Finnish *Jääkäri (Jäger)* are armed with the KK 62 (*konekivääri* 62, machine-gun model 1962) Finnish designed machine-gun and the RK 62 assault rifle, manufactured by Finnish companies Valmet and Sako based on the Polish licensed version of the Soviet AK-47 design. Their self-defence anti-tank weapon consists of the disposable 66 KES 75 (the US M72 LAW). Dedicated anti-tank teams use the 55 S 55 (55mm sinko vuodelta 1955, '55mm recoilless anti-tank weapon model 1955'), colloquially called *kevyt sinko* (light rocket launcher) and nicknamed *Nyrkki* (Fist). Though of a different design origin it is visually similar to the Soviet RPG-7. During the 1980s these were replaced with the more powerful French APILAS anti-tank weapon.

120 BTR-60s were delivered from the Soviet Union to Finland in 1976. These were operated by Finland's Jääkäri (Jäger) battalions.

SUOMEN MAAVOIMAT
BTR-60 TRANSPORT

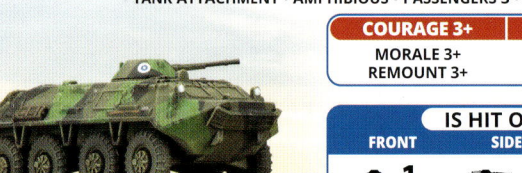

• TANK ATTACHMENT • AMPHIBIOUS • PASSENGERS 3 •

COURAGE 3+	SKILL 3+
MORALE 3+ REMOUNT 3+	ASSAULT 6 COUNTERATTACK 6

IS HIT ON 4+		
FRONT	SIDE	TOP
1	0	0

TACTICAL	TERRAIN DASH	CROSS COUNTRY DASH	ROAD DASH	CROSS
10"/25CM	10"/25CM	16"/40CM	36"/90CM	4+

WEAPON	RANGE	ROF HALTED	ROF MOVING	ANTI-TANK	FIRE-POWER	NOTES
14.5mm MG	20"/50CM	3	2	5	5+	
7.62mm MG	16"/40CM	1	1	2	6	

SUOMEN MAAVOIMAT
95 S 58-61 ANTI-TANK PLATOON

95 S 58-61 ANTI-TANK PLATOON
- 3x 95 S 58-61 recoilless rifle
- 3x BTR-60 (TFI112) — **4 POINTS**

OPTIONS
- Add up to 2x APILAS anti-tank team for +1 point each.

• INFANTRY UNIT •

COURAGE 3+	SKILL 3+
MORALE 3+ RALLY 3+	ASSAULT 5+ COUNTERATTACK 4+

IS HIT ON	INFANTRY SAVE
4+	3+

TACTICAL	TERRAIN DASH	CROSS COUNTRY DASH	ROAD DASH	CROSS
4"/10CM	4"/10CM	6"/15CM	8"/20CM	3+

WEAPON	RANGE	ROF HALTED	ROF MOVING	ANTI-TANK	FIRE-POWER	NOTES
95 S 58-61 recoilless rifle	24"/60CM	2	1	18	2+	Brutal, Forward Firing, HEAT, Heavy Weapon, Recoilless
OPTIONAL APILAS anti-tank team	16"/40CM	1	1	21	3+	HEAT, Slow Firing

The *95 S 58-61 raskas sinko* is a 95mm heavy recoilless anti-tank gun. It is also referred to colloquially as *Musti*. The gun was developed in 1958 and it was given a new wheeled carriage in 1961.

The weapon team consists of eight men: the team leader, gunner, loader/reserve gunner, two ammunition carriers, plus the reserve leader and two extra men armed with M72 LAWs and APILAS anti-tank weapons for close defense.

The group moves through the terrain to their firing position by running and pulling the weapon behind them, and this is popularly called "walking the Musti" (*Musti*, Blackie in English, is a stereotypical name for a black dog in Finnish).

FINNISH SUPPORT UNITS

SUOMEN MAAVOIMAT
BM-21 HAIL ROCKET LAUNCHER BATTERY

BM-21 HAIL ROCKET LAUNCHER BATTERY	
6x BM-21 Hail	13 POINTS
4x BM-21 Hail	8 POINTS
2x BM-21 Hail	4 POINTS

122 RakH 76, as the Soviet BM-21 Hail rocket launcher is known in Finnish Service, provides the Finns with rocket artillery.

• UNARMOURED TANK UNIT •

COURAGE 3+	SKILL 3+
MORALE 3+ RALLY 3+	ASSAULT - COUNTERATTACK -
IS HIT ON 4+	TANK SAVE 5+

TACTICAL	TERRAIN DASH	CROSS COUNTRY DASH	ROAD DASH	CROSS
8"/20cm	8"/20cm	14"/35cm	36"/90cm	4+

WEAPON	RANGE	ROF HALTED	ROF MOVING	ANTI-TANK	FIRE-POWER	NOTES
BM-21 rocket launcher	96"/240cm	SALVO		3	4+	Smoke Bombardment

SUOMEN MAAVOIMAT
2S1 CARNATION HOWITZER BATTERY

2S1 CARNATION HOWITZER BATTERY	
3x 2S1 Carnation	7 POINTS

In Finnish service the 2s1 Carnation is known as the 122 PsH 74 (*122 panssarihaupitsi 74*, 122mm armoured howitzer model 1974). They bought over 60 2s1 Carnations from the Soviet Union. They are used to support the mechansied brigades of the Finnish Army.

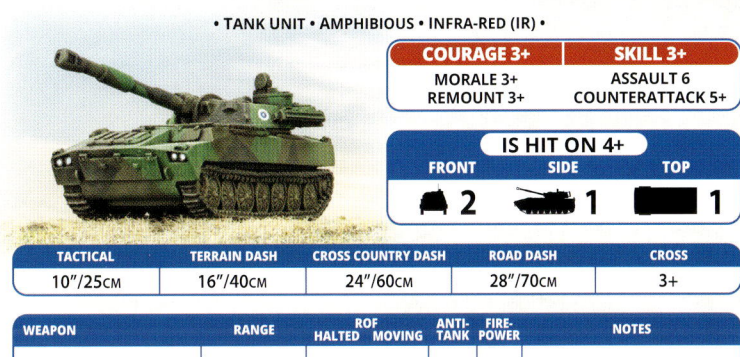

• TANK UNIT • AMPHIBIOUS • INFRA-RED (IR) •

COURAGE 3+	SKILL 3+
MORALE 3+ REMOUNT 3+	ASSAULT 6 COUNTERATTACK 5+

IS HIT ON 4+
FRONT	SIDE	TOP
2	1	1

TACTICAL	TERRAIN DASH	CROSS COUNTRY DASH	ROAD DASH	CROSS
10"/25cm	16"/40cm	24"/60cm	28"/70cm	3+

WEAPON	RANGE	ROF HALTED	ROF MOVING	ANTI-TANK	FIRE-POWER	NOTES
122mm 2A31 howitzer	88"/220cm	ARTILLERY		4	3+	Smoke Bombardment
or Direct fire	24"/60cm	1	1	21	2+	Brutal, HEAT, Slow Firing, Smoke

SUOMEN MAAVOIMAT
BMP-1 OP FORWARD OBSERVER

BMP-1 FORWARD OBSERVER	
1x BMP-1 OP	1 POINT

You must field:
- a 2s1 Carnation Howitzer Battery (TFI113), or
- a BM-21 Hail Rocket Launcher Battery (TFI121)

before you may field a BMP-1 OP Forward Observer.

The Finns use some of their BMP-1 infantry fighting vehicles as armoured observation posts for their artillery forward observers.

• INDEPENDENT TANK UNIT • AMPHIBIOUS • INFRA-RED (IR) • OBSERVER • SCOUT •

COURAGE 3+	SKILL 3+
MORALE 3+ REMOUNT 3+	ASSAULT 5+ COUNTERATTACK 5+

IS HIT ON 4+
FRONT	SIDE	TOP
2	2	1

TACTICAL	TERRAIN DASH	CROSS COUNTRY DASH	ROAD DASH	CROSS
10"/25cm	16"/40cm	28"/70cm	32"/80cm	3+

WEAPON	RANGE	ROF HALTED	ROF MOVING	ANTI-TANK	FIRE-POWER	NOTES
7.62mm MG	16"/40cm	3	3	2	6	

T-55 MARKSMAN ANTI-AIRCRAFT PLATOON
SUOMEN MAAVOIMAT

T-55 MARKSMAN ANTI-AIRCRAFT PLATOON
3x T-55 Marksman — **8 POINTS**

• TANK UNIT • INFRA-RED (IR) •

COURAGE 3+	SKILL 3+
MORALE 3+	ASSAULT 5+
REMOUNT 3+	COUNTERATTACK 5+

IS HIT ON 4+

FRONT	SIDE	TOP
5	3	1

TACTICAL	TERRAIN DASH	CROSS COUNTRY DASH	ROAD DASH	CROSS
10"/25CM	14"/35CM	20"/50CM	24"/60CM	4+

WEAPON	RANGE	ROF HALTED	ROF MOVING	ANTI-TANK	FIRE-POWER	NOTES
Twin 35mm L/90 gun	28"/70CM	5	4	11	4+	Dedicated AA, Radar

To replace the aging ZSU-57-2 AA tanks, the Finns fitted the British Marksman turret to the T-55 tank hull. The Marksman turret has proved to be a very accurate anti-aircraft artillery system, having a documented hit percentage of 52.44%.

It has a modern Marconi Series 400 anti-aircraft radar system and is armed with two Swiss Oerlikon 35mm anti-aircraft autocannons, giving it similar performance to the West German Gepard.

ZSU-57-2 ANTI-AIRCRAFT PLATOON
SUOMEN MAAVOIMAT

ZSU-57-2 ANTI-AIRCRAFT PLATOON
3x ZSU-57-2 — **3 POINTS**

Finland imported twelve ZSU-57-2 self-propelled anti-aircraft guns between 1960 and 1961. The Finnish designated the ZSU-57-2 as 57 ItPsv SU 57-2. They lack tracking and targeting radar so they only have limited utility against fast moving strike aircraft, but can be used to defeat enemy helicopters and provide additional ground support fire.

• TANK UNIT •

COURAGE 3+	SKILL 3+
MORALE 3+	ASSAULT 5+
REMOUNT 3+	COUNTERATTACK 5+

IS HIT ON 4+

FRONT	SIDE	TOP
2	1	0

TACTICAL	TERRAIN DASH	CROSS COUNTRY DASH	ROAD DASH	CROSS
10"/25CM	14"/35CM	20"/50CM	24"/60CM	3+

WEAPON	RANGE	ROF HALTED	ROF MOVING	ANTI-TANK	FIRE-POWER	NOTES
57mm Twin S-60 AA gun	24"/60CM	3	2	9	4+	Dedicated AA, Manual Tracking

ITO 78 ANTI-AIRCRAFT MISSILE PLATOON

SUOMEN MAAVOIMAT

ITO 78 ANTI-AIRCRAFT MISSILE PLATOON	
2x ITO 78 (SA-7 Grail) AA missile team	
1x BTR-60 (TFI112)	**3 POINTS**

Anti-aircraft (*Ilmatorjunta* in Finnish) cover was supplied by the attachment of an ITO 78 (*Ilmatorjuntaohjus* or Anti-aircraft Missile 78, Soviet SA-7B Grail) missile team.

• INFANTRY UNIT • HEAVY WEAPON •

COURAGE 3+	SKILL 3+
MORALE 3+ RALLY 3+	ASSAULT 6 COUNTERATTACK 4+

IS HIT ON	INFANTRY SAVE
4+	3+

TACTICAL	TERRAIN DASH	CROSS COUNTRY DASH	ROAD DASH	CROSS
8"/20CM	8"/20CM	12"/30CM	12"/30CM	AUTO

WEAPON	RANGE	HALTED	MOVING	ANTI-TANK	FIRE-POWER	NOTES
ITO 78 AA missile team	48"/120CM	3	-	-	5+	Guided AA

PSTOHJ ANTI-TANK MISSILE PLATOON

SUOMEN MAAVOIMAT

PSTOHJ ANTI-TANK MISSILE PLATOON	
4x PstOhj 83 (iTOW) missile team	
2x BMP-2 (TFI127)	**6 POINTS**
2x PstOhj 83 (iTOW) missile team	
1x BMP-2 (TFI127)	**3 POINTS**

Missile anti-tank capability comes from the American TOW (*PstOhj 83*) anti-tank missile systems. The improved TOW is very effective, but large and bulky.

Though often dismounted to be deployed in concealed ambush positions, they are best transported by an all-terrain vehicle. *PstOhj* is the Finnish military abbreviation of *Panssarintorjuntaohjus* (anti-tank missile).

• INFANTRY UNIT • HEAVY WEAPON • THERMAL IMAGING •

COURAGE 3+	SKILL 3+
MORALE 3+ RALLY 3+	ASSAULT - COUNTERATTACK -

IS HIT ON	INFANTRY SAVE
4+	3+

TACTICAL	TERRAIN DASH	CROSS COUNTRY DASH	ROAD DASH	CROSS
8"/20CM	8"/20CM	12"/30CM	12"/30CM	AUTO

WEAPON	RANGE	ROF HALTED	ROF MOVING	ANTI-TANK	FIRE-POWER	NOTES
PstOhj 83 (iTOW) missile	8"/20CM-48"/120CM	1	-	21	3+	Guided, HEAT

BMP-2 RECON PLATOON

SUOMEN MAAVOIMAT

BMP-2 RECON PLATOON	
3x BMP-2 Scout	**5 POINTS**

Some BMP-2 IFVs have been assigned to the reconnaissance role, proving protection for the scouts of the Recon Platoon (*Tiedustelujoukkue*) as they probe forward looking for the enemy.

The BMP-2 provides protection from light weapons and its 30mm cannon is more than enough to deal with opposing reconnaissance vehicles and infantry.

• TANK UNIT • AMPHIBIOUS • INFRA-RED (IR) • SCOUT • SPEARHEAD •

COURAGE 3+	SKILL 3+
MORALE 3+ REMOUNT 3+	ASSAULT 4+ COUNTERATTACK 5+

IS HIT ON 4+		
FRONT	SIDE	TOP
2	2	1

TACTICAL	TERRAIN DASH	CROSS COUNTRY DASH	ROAD DASH	CROSS
10"/25CM	16"/40CM	24"/60CM	32"/80CM	3+

WEAPON	RANGE	ROF HALTED	ROF MOVING	ANTI-TANK	FIRE-POWER	NOTES
30mm 2A42 gun	20"/50CM	3	2	10	5+	Anti-helicopter, Stabiliser
7.62mm MG	16"/40CM	3	3	2	6	
PstOhj 82M (AT-5) missile	8"/20CM-48"/120CM	1	-	21	3+	Guided, HEAT

FINNISH SUPPORT UNITS

FINNISH BASING & PAINTING

BASING FINNISH INFANTRY

Formation Command RK 62 team
Base the Commander on a small base with a radio operator and rifleman.

55 S 55 anti-tank team

APILAS anti-tank team
Base APILAS and 55 S 55 anti-tank teams on a small base with a gunner and an assistant.

KK PKM MG team with 66 KES 75 anti-tank

KK 62 MG team with 66 KES 75 anti-tank

Base Finnish Infantry teams on a medium base. Teams combine a machine-gunner armed with a light machine-gun (either KK PKM MGs or KK 62 MGs) and riflemen armed with rifles and light anti-tank weapons. Unit Leaders replace the machine-gun and a rifleman with an officer and radio operator.

81 KRH 71 mortar team

PstOhj 83 (iTOW) missile team

95 S 58-61 recoilless rifle team

Base 95 S 58-61 recoilless rifle teams, 81mm KRH 71 mortar teams, and PstOhj 83 (iTOW) missile teams on a medium base. Teams combine a weapon and three crew.

ITO 78 (SA-7 Grail) AA missile team
Base ITO 78 AA missile teams on a large base with three AA missile gunners and three rifle-armed assistants.

120mm KRH 73 mortar team
Base 120mm KRH 73 mortar teams on a large base with a 120mm mortar and four mortar crew.

Finnish Infantry

Flesh
Flat Flesh (955)

Beige Brown (875)

Uniform Base
Flat Earth (983)

Camouflage Colour
Luftwaffe Cam. Green (823)

Camouflage Colour
Dark Yellow (978)

Webbing
Khaki (988)

Rifle Magazines
Oily Steel (865)

Painted Metal
Cam. Olive Green (894)

Boots and RK Rifles
Black Grey (862)

Finnish Vehicles

Russian Uniform 924

Black Grey 862

Uniform Green 922

FINNISH CATALOGUE

The following pages contain a catalogue of all the miniatures that are available to a Finnish force.

Finnish forces use products from the following nations' catalogues:

 FINNISH  SOVIET  IRAQI

TNA950 — FINNISH SWEDISH NORWEGIAN DANISH

Nordic Forces Decals

Finnish Unit Cards — **WW3-08F**

26x Finnish Unit Cards, and
7x Swedish Allied Support Unit Cards.

World War III Team Yankee — FINNISH UNIT CARD PACK

TSBX29

T-72FM1

T-72FM2

ALL PLASTIC

CONTAINS:
5x T-72FM1 or T-72FM2 Tanks

SOVIET — **T-72 Tank Company**

TSBX07

CONTAINS:
3x 2S1 Carnation Self-propelled Howitzers

SOVIET — **2S1 Carnation Battery**

TSBX22

CONTAINS:
5x T-55M Tanks

SOVIET — T-55AM Tank Company

TSBX08

CONTAINS:
3x BM-21 Hail Rocket Launchers

SOVIET — BM-21 Hail Battery

TQBX03

CONTAINS:
2x ZSU-57-2 Anti-aircraft Tank

IRAQI — ZSU-57-2 AA Company

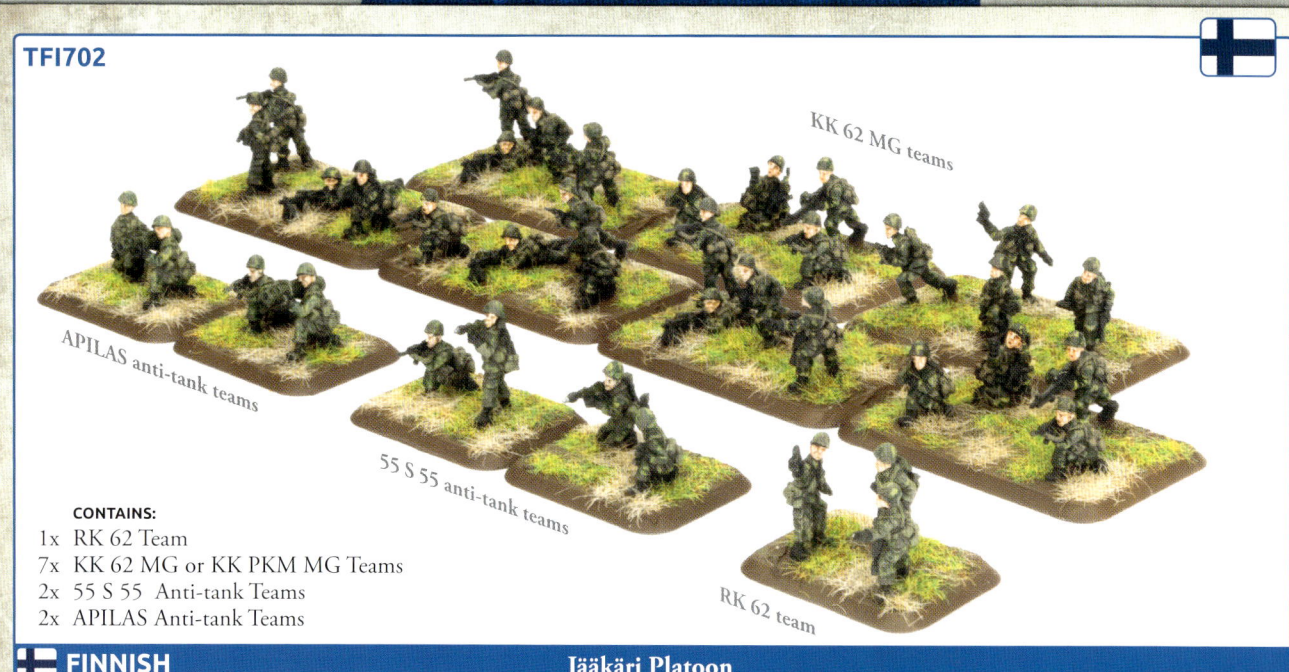

TFI702

CONTAINS:
- 1x RK 62 Team
- 7x KK 62 MG or KK PKM MG Teams
- 2x 55 S 55 Anti-tank Teams
- 2x APILAS Anti-tank Teams

FINNISH — Jääkäri Platoon

TFI703

CONTAINS:
- 3x 95 S 58-61 Recoilless Rifle Teams
- 2x APILAS Anti-tank Teams
- 2x ITO 78 (SA-7 Grail) AA Missile Teams
- 4x PstOhj 83 (iTOW) Missile Teams

FINNISH — Weapons Platoons

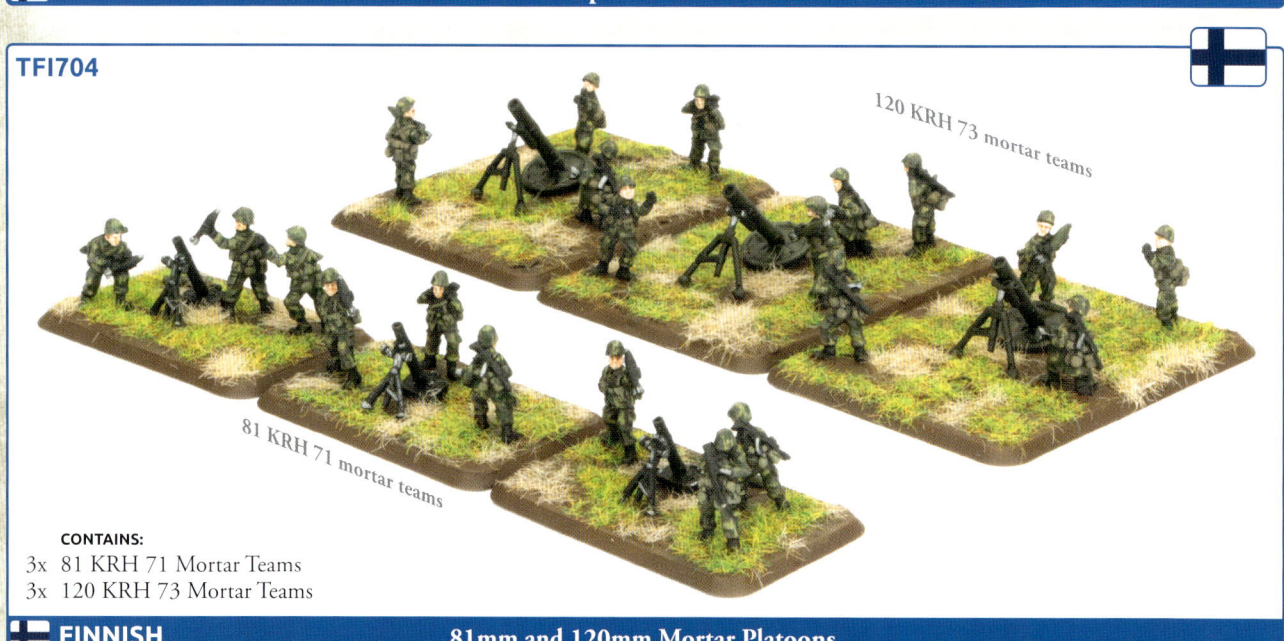

TFI704

CONTAINS:
- 3x 81 KRH 71 Mortar Teams
- 3x 120 KRH 73 Mortar Teams

FINNISH — 81mm and 120mm Mortar Platoons

TSBX02

BMP-1

BMP-2

CONTAINS:
5x BMP-1 or BMP-2 Transports

SOVIET — BMP-1 or BMP-2 Company

TSBX14

CONTAINS:
5x BTR-60 Transports

SOVIET — BTR-60 Transport Platoon

TFIBX01

CONTAINS:
3x T-55 Marksman Anti-aircraft Tanks

FINNISH — T-55 Marksman Platoon

35

FORCES IN WORLD WAR III

Sweden was able to successfully maintain neutrality throughout World War II, sparing it conquest and occupation by Germany or any other foreign power. This was the main reasons for its exceptional prosperity after the war, backed up by American economic support (through the Marshall Plan).

The key influences that shapped Swedish military policy during the Cold War was its political neutrality and its strategic location in the front line with the Soviet Union. This lead to Sweden developing very strong coastal defence and a powerful air force. Sweden's military aim was to create a credible deterrent and prevent a Soviet attack. However, Sweden was prepared for total war in case of an attack from the Soviet Union.

Sweden was also mostly self-sufficient in much of its military equipment such as artillery and aircraft.

SWEDISH NEUTRALITY

Though Sweden was officially neutral, it maintained close contact with both the United States and NATO to the point of cooperation. It would have been impossible for Sweden to be neutral in the case of a war between NATO and the Warsaw Pact. In fact, the Swedish military forces were directed openly against the Soviet Union. The only realistic and successful possibility of defending Sweden in case of war was on the basis of support from the United States. Military ties with NATO were therefore kept secret by the Swedish government because of its official policy of neutrality.

SWEDEN'S STRATEGIC LOCATION

Most Soviet attack plans throughout the Cold War period involved the Nordic countries. The Soviets desired military control over and access to the North Atlantic. The Soviet Union also wanted to control access to the Baltic Sea and any all-weather ports.

Sweden sat across half of the frontier between Western Europe and the Eastern Bloc. Control of this border led to many confrontations between Swedish and Soviet aircraft in the Baltic Sea, including the downing of a Swedish surveillance aircraft in 1952 (known as the DC-3 affair).

Other confrontations involved Soviet submarines. One of these submarines, the U137, ran ashore in 1981 inside the restricted zone of the Karlskrona Naval Base, and resulted in a brief political crisis between Sweden and the Soviet Union.

COASTAL DEFENCE

The eastern coast of Sweden, along a length of more than 1500 kilometres, probably had the most powerful coastal defence system in the world. The system consisted of coastal artillery, submarines, warships, and aircraft.

No less than 90 coastal guns (typically 7.5cm calibre) serviced by large underground facilities were strategically located along the coast, supplemented by a large number of bunkers and pillboxes.

AIR FORCE

Sweden had the fourth largest air force in the world, with no less than 30 bases and a large number of smaller hangars mainly connected to motorways that could be used as runways in case of war. One of the main tasks of the Swedish air force was to hinder attacks from Soviet anti-submarine flights against NATO missile submarines in the Baltic Sea.

THE ARMY

Due to the increased tensions of the Cold War the size of the Swedish Army (*Svenska Armén*) grew considerably. Between 1950 and 1976 it grew to around 250,000 soldiers, with a peak of 400,000 mobilisable soldiers during the late 1950s and early 1960s. However, though national service was compulsory and failure to serve was punishable by imprisonment, service was not heavily enforced.

In the 1980s, the army consisted of a large number of field units, local defence units, and home guards. The field units consisted of mobilisation commands with staff and liaison units, about 50 independent infantry, armoured, artillery and air defense battalions, 24 infantry and Norrland brigades (units organised for roadless terrain mounted in various all-terrain vehicles introduced in 1985). Four armoured brigades and a mechanised brigade made up the bulk of the capability.

The local defense units consisted of about 100 battalions and 400-500 independent companies. In total, the Army was able to mobilise about 600,000 men, of which the Home Guard (*Hemvärnet*) contributed almost 100,000 men.

SWEDEN & WORLD WAR III

Like NATO and the other neutral nations, Sweden was critically aware of the building tensions between the west and the Soviet block. Sweden began mobilising its defence forces as early as the end of June 1985 as US forces began readying to reinforce their units in West Germany. The Swedish Air Force had stepped up active patrolling and Coastal Forces were on high alert.

When Soviet forces crossed the Finnish and Norwegian borders on 7 August, Sweden immediately announced its intent to offer assistance to Finland, denouncing the Soviet Union's blatant breach of a fellow neutral nation's sovereignty.

Immediately, the Swedish Air Force's ground attack squadrons began flying sorties in support of the Finnish ground forces. The Swedish Army's anti-tank helicopter units also began flying in support of the Finns, while the northern Swedish brigades moved towards the Finnish frontier.

PERSSON'S CENTURIONS

This was never supposed to happen. *Löjtnant* Karl Persson never for a moment believed that the Soviet Union was Sweden's friend – in fact Russia and Sweden had traditionally been bitter enemies. Yet his nation had managed to tread the careful line of neutrality. When World War II engulfed the world, Sweden was the only Scandinavian country to escape the horrors of that conflict. With the coming of the Cold War, Sweden pursued a policy of armed neutrality. Conventional wisdom held that should one of the superpowers start a third World War, the Soviets would simply bypass and isolate Finland, Norway, and Sweden in a desire to control the North Atlantic. Apparently, the Soviets decided Gotland and its defences represented a threat to their overall war plans.

Löjtnant Persson had been stationed on Gotland for over a year commanding his Stridsvagn 104 tank, one of the upgraded versions of the British Centurion with explosive reactive armour, as part of the Gotland Brigade's 2nd Armoured Battalion. Gotland had always held enormous strategic importance, and Sweden had fortified it.

With the Soviet attack on NATO in early August 1985, the Gotland Military Command had been on high alert and both naval and air reconnaissance patrols had been beefed up accordingly. Soviet naval traffic through the Baltic Sea had been heavy with vessels of all types moving west to support the overall offensive. Tensions had been high – especially as both sides had attempted to fire cruise missiles through Swedish air space. That all changed on August 30 when several Soviet Ropucha class landing ships, which had appeared to be heading south toward Germany or Denmark, abruptly changed course and made a beeline for Gotland's east coast.

In a well-coordinated attack, Soviet naval and air assets began pounding Swedish positions on Gotland. Cruise missiles struck the air bases at Bunge, Roma, and Visby, but Persson knew that many of the Air Force's Viggen aircraft had already been dispersed to improvised airfields. So, when the order came to mobilise his battalion to move to oppose the Soviet amphibious assault, he hoped that there would at least be some available air support.

By the time the 2nd Armoured Battalion made it the few kilometers from Visby to their assigned defence sector near the village of Åminne, the Soviets already had main battle tanks, armoured personnel carriers, and substantial infantry assets ashore. Scattered radio traffic indicated that additional amphibious or airborne attacks may be underway on other parts of the island, but with the enemy in front of them the 2nd Armoured Battalion already had its hands full. Of primary concern to the tankers were the Soviet T-72B tanks that had rapidly formed a battle line and began cutting through the 18th Armoured Reconnaissance Company before they could disengage. Several of the Soviet tanks had been hit by anti-tank missiles, but only one appeared to have been knocked out because of the updated reactive armour.

Löjtnant Persson knew conventional wisdom often held that any invasion should be stopped at the shore, but he also knew charging a company of Strv 104s right into the teeth of the Soviet machines would be suicidal. While his Stridsvagn tanks' 105mm guns would struggle in a head-to-head engagement with Soviet armour, their 125mm guns would make mincemeat of his tanks in the same engagement. His company's only chance against the enemy armour was to draw them inland where the Stridsvagns could get flanking shots and the accuracy of their L7 guns could be used to best advantage. Persson directed his armour south towards Gothem where his tank company and the rest of the 2nd Battalion would set up defensive positions to hopefully catch the advancing Soviets in a crossfire.

GOTHEM

Persson dispersed his dozen tanks in wooded areas surrounding the fields of Gothem. The crews quickly worked to camouflage their vehicles as best as possible before the inevitable Soviet push inland. Persson could hear Battalion artillery pounding the Soviet bridgehead, and scattered reports on the radio indicated the Soviets were trying to move both north and west from the bridgehead. Persson could also see the Battalion's infantry which was digging in across the area. The two companies of 90mm recoilless rifles were also scattered through the area, invisible for the time being, but they'd become all too obvious once they opened fire on any advancing Soviets

After a wait which seemed like an eternity, lookouts reported Soviet elements moving south down the road toward Gothem in the early afternoon. Four T-72B tanks backed up by a few BTRs were probing south. It was clear they'd seen the Swedish infantry in front of the settlement as they drew

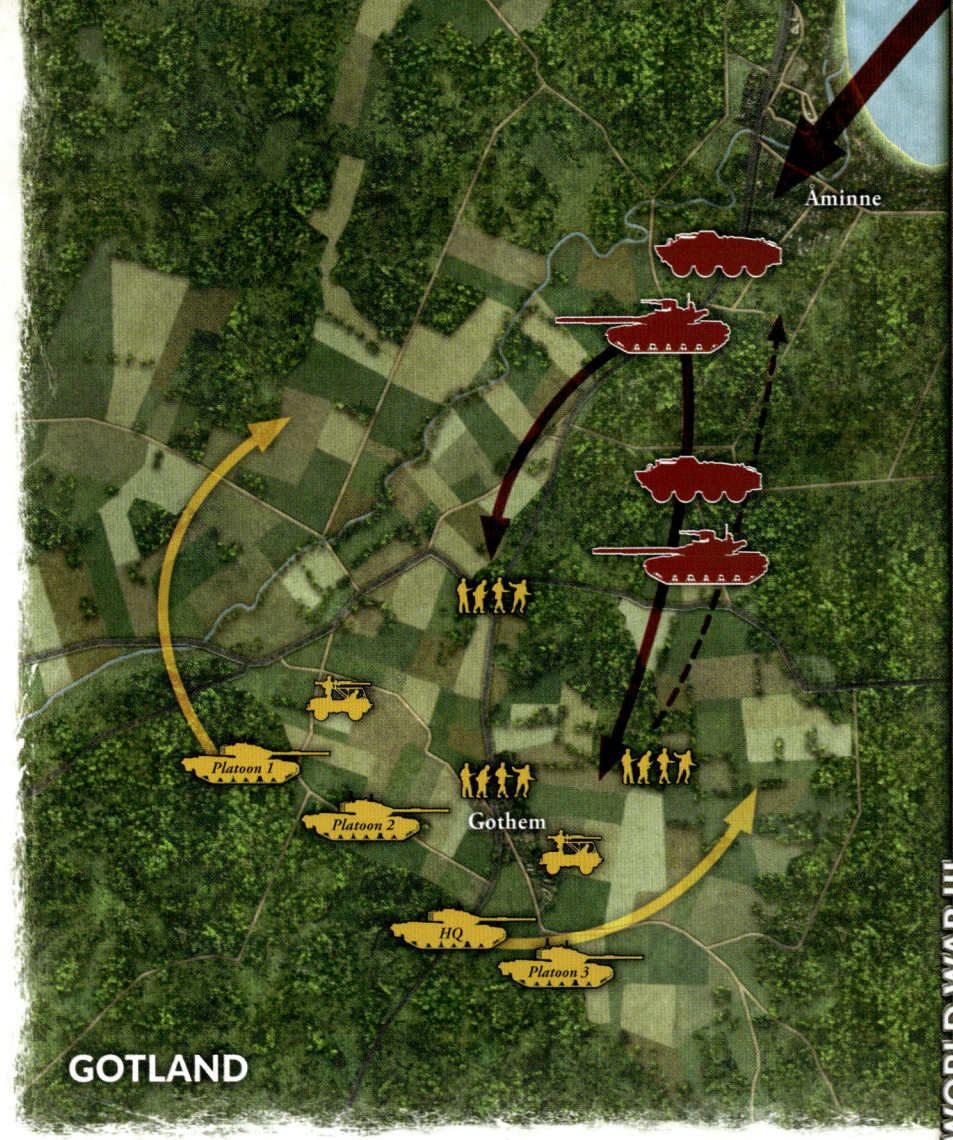

to a halt. All units were ordered to hold fire until the full makeup of the enemy force was clear. Seconds after that order came through, all hell broke loose. Soviet artillery began pounding the Swedish positions in front of Gothem. One of Persson's platoons of tanks reported eight more T-72s and additional BTRs moving through the wooded area to the northeast in an attempt to flank the settlement. With the window of opportunity rapidly closing, Persson gave the order for his tanks to engage, and the rest of the Battalion followed suit.

The four visible T-72B tanks were the highest priority, and Persson and at least three of his tanks had good flanking shots on them. The 105mm guns opened fire and within a minute, three of the Soviet machines were burning. The fourth tank managed to get shots off and destroyed one Swedish tank before it was in turn destroyed by a round from a previously hidden 90mm recoilless gun. With the loss of their armoured support, the BTRs turned tail and retreated. To the northeast, however, the situation was more desperate. Persson could hear the chaotic battle progress on the radio as four Strv 104s and two or three 90mm guns with light infantry support were facing at least eight T-72Bs, BTRs and infantry.

Persson ordered the surviving tanks from around the settlement to relieve the defenders to the northeast in a rough pincer formation with his platoon of three tanks moving east and the other platoon coming from the south. Hopefully between the two pincers there would be enough crossfire to blunt the attack. Once they arrived, the battlefield was a scene of extreme carnage. Three T-72B tanks had been knocked out, but all four Stridsvagn and at least two 90mm guns had been destroyed.

The infantry was falling back in good order attempting to hold up the Soviet advance with anti-tank missiles.

Before the Soviet battle tanks could regroup, Persson and his fresh tanks opened fire. Many shots bounced harmlessly off the front armor of the Soviet tanks, but in turning to respond to one threat, the Soviets opened themselves up to flanking shots. After a few minutes of intense fighting three more Soviet tanks had been destroyed and the rest withdrew north back toward the bridgehead. Gothem had been held, but the cost had been high. Six of the Battalion's twelve tanks had been knocked out along with two of their recoilless guns. Infantry casualties had been relatively light, but Persson knew that Sweden could never win a battle of attrition against the Soviets.

SVENSKA ARMÉN
SWEDISH FORCE

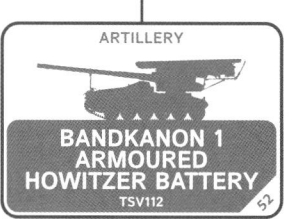

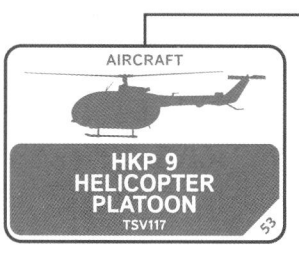
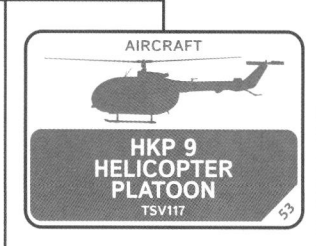

NATO ALLIED FORMATION
YOU MAY FIELD ONE NATO FORMATION AS AN ALLIED FORMATION

FORMATION SUPPORT
You may field compulsory Combat Units (with a black box) from the above Formations as Support Units.

NATO ALLIED SUPPORT

Sweden is officially neutral, but like Finland, they stand in the path of any Soviet thrust towards Norway, a member of the NATO alliance. Any intrusion into their national territory would likely result in them siding with NATO forces fighting the Warsaw Pact.

You may take a NATO Allied Formation as part of your Force. A NATO Allied Formation can be from any other Force with a NATO Allied Formation in its support.

An Allied Formation obeys all the rules for its own nationality. An Allied Formation Commander can only join Units in its own Formation or nation and only its Formation or national Units can benefit from its Command Leadership (see page 25 and 64 of *World War III: Team Yankee*).

An Allied Formation does not count as a Formation when determining if you have lost the game (see page 65 of *World War III: Team Yankee*).

FINNISH ALLIED SUPPORT

ARMOUR

- T-72FM1 ARMOURED PLATOON — TFI102 — 15
- T-72FM2 ARMOURED PLATOON — TFI104 — 17
- T-55M ARMOURED PLATOON — TFI106 — 19

INFANTRY
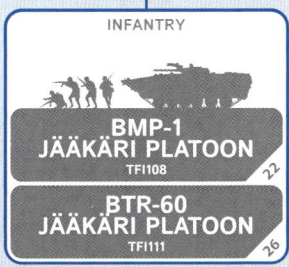
- BMP-1 JÄÄKÄRI PLATOON — TFI108 — 22
- BTR-60 JÄÄKÄRI PLATOON — TFI111 — 26

ARTILLERY
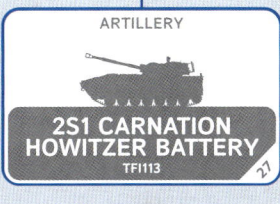
- 2S1 CARNATION HOWITZER BATTERY — TFI113 — 27

Rules for Finnish Formations and Units can be found on pages 12 to 29 of this book.

SWEDISH SPECIAL RULES

The Swedish Army has a number of features and weapons. These are reflected in the following special rules.

ACCURATE
The Bofors 90mm recoilless anti-tank gun is fitted with a modified rifle as ranging or spotting rifle.

> If stationary, a Team Weapon with Accurate has no To Hit penalty for shooting at ranges over 16"/40cm.

AMBUSH TANK
Though the S-Tank is primarily intened as a main battle tank, to be equally at home in offensive and defensive actions, its low silhouette and hydropneumatic suspension made it particularly good in defence among the wooded terrain of Sweden.

> If stationary, a Team with the Ambush Tank rule can remain Gone to Ground while shooting its main gun.

AUTOLOADER
Like the French AMX AuF1 155mm howitzer, the Swedish Bandkanon 1 self-propelled 155mm howitzer is fitted with an auto-loading system, allowing it to lay down quick devastating barrages.

> When a weapon with an Autoloader fires an Artillery Bombardment reduce the score required To Hit Teams under the Template by 1.

OVERWORKED
The Swedish S-Tank does not have a stabiliser so relies on short halts while firing on the move. This requires well-drilled coordination between the driver/gunner and commander.

> Overworked weapons add +1 to the score needed To Hit when moving.

SLAT ARMOUR
The Swedish S-Tank mounted slat bar armour on its front hull and used "Jerry" fuel cans as a form of spaced armour side skirts.

> Teams with Slat Armour have a Front and Side Armour rating of 13 against HEAT weapons.

STRV 103 S-TANK TANK COMPANY

Löjtnant Klas Andersson checked his watch and then heard the "pop, pop, pop" of the preliminary bombardment. "Right on time... now the 104s should start attacking from the south."

Andersson saw the Soviets slewing their turrets to the south. The older Centurions had borne the brunt of the fighting, but the Soviets had grown accustomed to their flanking tactics. He could see a few T-72Bs take hits, but none appeared to be knocked out. However, while a few tanks were still pointed in his direction, most were now reacting to the southern threat.

"Our turn..." Andersson mused. He keyed his radio, "second platoon, move up once we hit the tanks facing us."

Andersson quickly assessed the situation, at least 20 T-72B tanks in the field, with roughly 14 of them focused on the 104s to the south. His company of twelve tanks would first take out the six watching tanks from the west. He assigned the targets by platoon.

Andersson keyed the radio again, "All tanks, open fire!"

The 105mm gun of the S tank roared to life causing the entire vehicle to shudder. Andersson could see that four of the T-72s had brewed up, but the others were now starting to fire in this direction.

"Second platoon move up, first and third platoons provide covering fire."

The three S-tanks from second platoon darted from their prepared cover to another copse of trees roughly 100 metres to the northeast. As expected, the Soviets focused their attention on the visible targets, and began to manoeuvre across the open terrain. One of the tanks of second platoon was hit, but the suspension appeared to absorb most of the shot. The tank didn't brew up, but the crew bailed out.

Nilsson, and the rest of first and third platoons had not been idle, though. Two more T-72Bs were burning.

Andersson looked south where several smoke plumes grew on the horizon, "It looks like the 104s aren't making much headway." He keyed the radio again, "third platoon, second platoon, cover fire while first advances."

Andersson's platoon made a mad dash for a small group of trees and buildings to engage the Soviets.

The armoured troops of the Swedish Army were organised into mixed *Mekaniserad Bataljoner* (Mechanised Battalions). These consisted of two mechanised infantry companies (*mekaniserade skyttekompanier*) and two tank companies (*stridsvagnskompanier*), as well as battalion command, services, and a small howitzer company.

The concept of the mixed all-arms formation was introduced with the Armoured Brigade 63 reforms. Hilly and forested Swedish terrain often meant that it was difficult to get long-range weapons to shoot at the same target. Companies and battalions were therefore usually the largest units that could conduct integrated combat, so these units would need to have a diverse composition.

The requirement for speed of deployment and readiness for action was also considered when introducing the mixed battalions. The experience with the previous organisation with separate purely tank and armoured infantry battalions, was that they often required temporary attachment of infantry to the tank battalion and vise versa. Such contingencies took time to organise and went against the requirement to be able to attack directly from the march. On the other hand, temporarily gathering tank companies into a tank battalion could be done relatively quickly thanks to the uniformity of their organisation and communication systems.

A tank company, or *Stridsvagnskompani*, was made up of four tank platoons (*Stridsvagnspluton*) and an armoured infantry platoon (*Pansarskyttepluton*). In the field they would be attached weapons and other platoons from the battalion and brigade as required.

The S-tank is a unique design, using it's tracks to traverse the gun rather than a more conventional turret. To raise or lower the gun the S-tank uses its unique suspension. This resaults in a tank with a very low profile design that can make the most use of small folds in the ground, only showing the gun and a fraction of the hull as a possible target for enemy fire.

If you want to model your S-Tanks this way, visit the *Team-Yankee* website and purchase the code: **TSWSO01 – S-Tank Tracks.**

SVENSKA ARMÉN
STRV 103 S-TANK TANK COMPANY

You must field the Formation HQ and one Combat Unit from each black box.
You may also field one Combat Unit from each grey box.

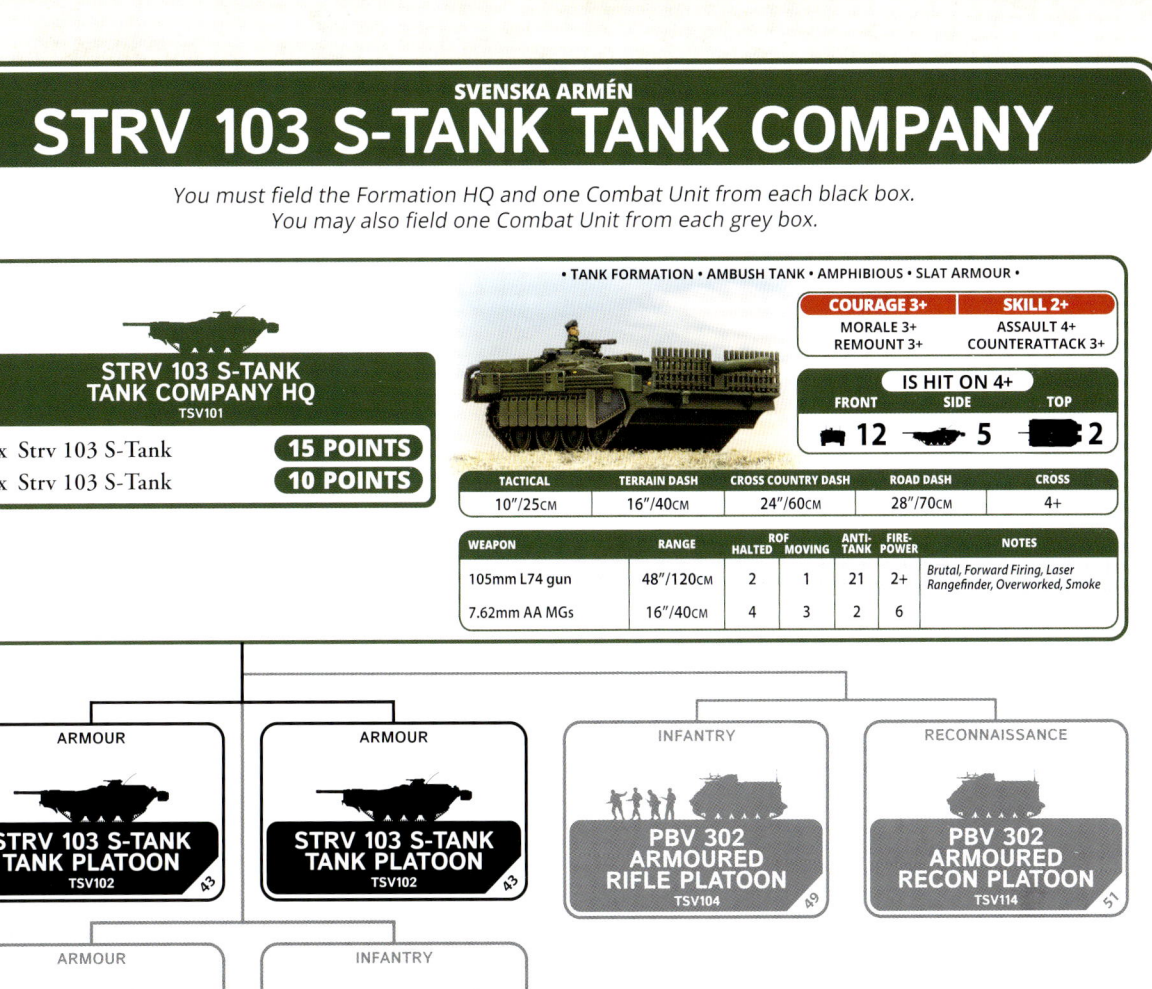

• TANK FORMATION • AMBUSH TANK • AMPHIBIOUS • SLAT ARMOUR •

STRV 103 S-TANK TANK COMPANY HQ — TSV101
- 3x Strv 103 S-Tank — 15 POINTS
- 2x Strv 103 S-Tank — 10 POINTS

COURAGE 3+	SKILL 2+
MORALE 3+	ASSAULT 4+
REMOUNT 3+	COUNTERATTACK 3+

IS HIT ON 4+
FRONT 12 | SIDE 5 | TOP 2

TACTICAL	TERRAIN DASH	CROSS COUNTRY DASH	ROAD DASH	CROSS
10"/25CM	16"/40CM	24"/60CM	28"/70CM	4+

WEAPON	RANGE	ROF HALTED	ROF MOVING	ANTI-TANK	FIRE-POWER	NOTES
105mm L74 gun	48"/120CM	2	1	21	2+	Brutal, Forward Firing, Laser Rangefinder, Overworked, Smoke
7.62mm AA MGs	16"/40CM	4	3	2	6	

ARMOUR — STRV 103 S-TANK TANK PLATOON (TSV102) [black]
ARMOUR — STRV 103 S-TANK TANK PLATOON (TSV102) [black]
INFANTRY — PBV 302 ARMOURED RIFLE PLATOON (TSV104) [grey]
RECONNAISSANCE — PBV 302 ARMOURED RECON PLATOON (TSV114) [grey]
ARMOUR — STRV 103 S-TANK TANK PLATOON (TSV102) [grey]
INFANTRY — PBV 302 ARMOURED RIFLE PLATOON (TSV104) [grey]

You may field a Combat Unit from a black box as a Support Unit for your Force.

SVENSKA ARMÉN
STRV 103 S-TANK TANK PLATOON

STRV 103 S-TANK TANK PLATOON
- 3x Strv 103 S-Tank — 15 POINTS

• TANK UNIT • AMBUSH TANK • AMPHIBIOUS • SLAT ARMOUR •

COURAGE 4+	SKILL 3+
MORALE 4+	ASSAULT 4+
REMOUNT 3+	COUNTERATTACK 4+

IS HIT ON 4+
FRONT 12 | SIDE 5 | TOP 2

TACTICAL	TERRAIN DASH	CROSS COUNTRY DASH	ROAD DASH	CROSS
10"/25CM	16"/40CM	24"/60CM	28"/70CM	4+

WEAPON	RANGE	ROF HALTED	ROF MOVING	ANTI-TANK	FIRE-POWER	NOTES
105mm L74 gun	48"/120CM	2	1	21	2+	Brutal, Forward Firing, Laser Rangefinder, Overworked, Smoke
7.62mm AA MGs	16"/40CM	4	3	2	6	

Developed in the 1950s, then modernised in the 1980s, the *Stridsvagn 103* S-Tank is the first main battle tank to use a turbine engine and to dispense with a turret. This unconventional design has a unique gun laying process: its fixed gun is traversed by engaging the tracks and elevated by adjusting the hull suspension. The result was a very low-profile design with an emphasis on survivability and heightened crew protection level.

It is also fitted with an autoloader to reduce its crew size and replicated controls so that the commander or gunner may drive the tank and fire the main gun. A third crewman is a radio operator/driver and sits in a rearward facing position from where they have another set of driving controls for rapid re-deployment.

While the Strv 103 S-Tank cannot fire while moving, the autoloader combined with short halt firing tactics allow it to fight well on the advance.

STRV 104 CENTURION TANK COMPANY

Löjtnant Stefan Bergstörm's Battalion was assigned one of the best defensive positions in north Gotland between Närs and Tingstäde. The area included quarries, marshland, lakes, as well as broken hills. With their artillery and infantry digging in, his tanks took up an ambush position and remained in contact with the rest of the company. Smoke on the southern horizon indicated that the fight had already begun, and there were reports that the 3rd Armoured Battalion had been overrun.

Noting movement along the road running south, Bergstörm swore a silent oath as he saw Soviet T-72 tanks come into view. He immediately contacted the rest of the Battalion on the radio, "all crews, contact, south. T-72s, remember your training. Hold fire until you have favourable shots."

"Iver, you're one of the best shots in the whole command, stay sharp."

The gunner did not flinch and merely said, "I've already got their lead tank lined up, sir. It's like they think we don't have any reserves."

Bergstörm took another glance through his periscope. Iver was right. It looked like rather than continuing north through the nature preserve and rough terrain, the Soviets were turning toward Närs along a narrow track of road between the bog and the sea.

Bergstörm was immediately back on the radio "All units hold fire until most of that group is on the road, I'll then hit the lead tank – Engström, you hit the trailing one, then all tanks unleash hell on the rest."

Within minutes, eight Soviet main battle tanks were on the narrow road. With the firing arc as good as they were going to get, Bergtörm gave the order, "take the shot, Iver"

"Firing now."

Iver's shot was true, striking the flank of the Soviet tank and Lars, his loader, had immediately ensured the breech was clear and another round was ready to fire. Within a minute, all eight of the Soviet tanks were burning, never having seen the Stridsvagn that had hit them.

Production of the Strv 103A S-Tank began in 1967. The appearance of the Strv 103 did not mean that the Centurion would retire. It was decided that the more conventional Centurion would be a superior option for certain tasks. The Centurion upgrade program to up-gun to the 105mm L7 gun and add extra armour *(Strv 101* and *Strv 102)* did not come without expense, but it did extended the life in those British tanks.

The *Strv 101* and *Strv 102* were planned to be replaced by a tank designed as a part of the MBT 2000 program, but it did not progress past a full scale model. Meanwhile, Bofors performed the next stage of modernisation from 1983 *(Strv 101R* and *102R)* where they received new electronics, new lights, a pair of smoke mortars added to the roof, and explosive reactive armour (ERA), similar to the Blazer armour developed by the Israeli company RAFAEL.

The final variant was the *Strv 104*, developed after studying the modernisation of Centurion tanks in other countries. These tanks received better reactive armour than the *Strv 101R* and *102R*. Hägglunds & Söner AB, who undertook the upgrades, also improved the mobility by taking the same route as the Israelis by fitting the same gearbox and powerful diesel engine as the American M60 tank. This increased the tank's top speed to 48 km/h and improved reliability. The *Strv 104* turret also received new fire control systems.

STRV 104 CENTURION TANK COMPANY
SVENSKA ARMÉN

You must field the Formation HQ and one Combat Unit from each black box.
You may also field one Combat Unit from each grey box.

• TANK FORMATION • ERA • INFRA-RED (IR) •

STRV 104 CENTURION TANK COMPANY HQ
TSV107

3x Strv 104 Centurion		**9 POINTS**
2x Strv 104 Centurion		**6 POINTS**

COURAGE 3+	SKILL 2+
MORALE 3+	ASSAULT 4+
REMOUNT 3+	COUNTERATTACK 3+

IS HIT ON 4+

FRONT	SIDE	TOP
14	6	2

TACTICAL	TERRAIN DASH	CROSS COUNTRY DASH	ROAD DASH	CROSS
10"/25cm	12"/30cm	18"/45cm	18"/45cm	2+

WEAPON	RANGE	ROF HALTED	ROF MOVING	ANTI-TANK	FIRE-POWER	NOTES
105mm L7 gun	40"/100cm	2	1	19	2+	Brutal, Laser Rangefinder, Smoke, Stabliser
7.62mm AA MG	16"/40cm	3	3	2	6	
7.62mm MG	16"/40cm	1	1	2	6	

ARMOUR — STRV 104 CENTURION TANK PLATOON — TSV108 — 45

ARMOUR — STRV 104 CENTURION TANK PLATOON — TSV108 — 45

INFANTRY — PBV 302 ARMOURED RIFLE PLATOON — TSV104 — 49

RECONNAISSANCE — PBV 302 ARMOURED RECON PLATOON — TSV114 — 51

ARMOUR — STRV 104 CENTURION TANK PLATOON — TSV108 — 45

INFANTRY — PBV 302 ARMOURED RIFLE PLATOON — TSV104 — 49

You may field a Combat Unit from a black box as a Support Unit for your Force.

STRV 104 CENTURION TANK PLATOON
SVENSKA ARMÉN

STRV 104 CENTURION TANK PLATOON

3x Strv 104 Centurion	**9 POINTS**

• TANK UNIT • ERA • INFRA-RED (IR) •

COURAGE 4+	SKILL 3+
MORALE 4+	ASSAULT 4+
REMOUNT 3+	COUNTERATTACK 4+

IS HIT ON 4+

FRONT	SIDE	TOP
14	6	2

TACTICAL	TERRAIN DASH	CROSS COUNTRY DASH	ROAD DASH	CROSS
10"/25cm	12"/30cm	18"/45cm	18"/45cm	2+

WEAPON	RANGE	ROF HALTED	ROF MOVING	ANTI-TANK	FIRE-POWER	NOTES
105mm L7 gun	40"/100cm	2	1	19	2+	Brutal, Laser Rangefinder, Smoke, Stabliser
7.62mm AA MG	16"/40cm	3	3	2	6	
7.62mm MG	16"/40cm	1	1	2	6	

The Swedes have been using the British Centurion since 1953. By the 1980s upgrade programs have modernised the fleet and all tanks are armed with the 105mm L7 rifled gun. The Strv 104 Centurions are equipped with new sights and an improved fire control system. They have had the old petrol engine replaced by the engine and transmission from the American M60, comprising an air-cooled diesel engine and a semi-automatic gearbox.

The Strv 104 inherited the Mark 10 Centurion's 120mm thick sloped armour. To this have been added Explosive Reactive Armour (ERA) blocks that cover the glacis front, part of the turret ring, front, mantlet and turret roof.

The Strv 104 Centurion is well liked; the new gearbox makes it very easy to drive compared to its predecessor, and the top speed has increased to 48km/h (from 35km/h).

ARMOURED RIFLE COMPANY

In the early afternoon, Swedish artillery opened up on the Soviet positions. Löjtnant Halvar Lindberg could see many of the Soviet tanks turn their attention south towards the known threat, but at least four T-72 tanks as well as several BMP-2s with their dismounted infantry began scanning the northern approaches. It appeared that Ivan had learned from his previous encounters with the Swedish defenders.

"Korpral Nilsson, are our little surprises for those tanks ready?"

"Yes, Löjtnant – the teams are set up and ready to fire on your order."

"Just make sure they fire at different tanks – it wouldn't do to waste all of them on one machine."

"Sir!"

Lindberg keyed his radio, "All platoons, stand by to advance once BILL introduces himself to Ivan. BILL teams, FIRE!"

From their improvised positions in the forest, three missiles streaked out toward the T-72 tanks representing the greatest threat to the armoured infantry teams. The advanced missiles initially looked like they would miss the defending tanks but instead detonated above the enemy tanks, as intended, knocking three of them out immediately. Lindberg noted that the top-attack mode of the BILL made the new light weapons as effective as the heavier TOW missiles.

"All teams advance, BILL and anti-tank teams, fire at will!"

Stunned by the loss of three tanks, the Soviets took a moment to react to the advancing Swedes. The battle soon developed into a short-ranged firefight that negated some of the Soviet firepower advantage. Swedish troops, with superior knowledge of the terrain, moved from house to house keeping Soviet infantry guessing, knocking out the remaining tank and five BMP armoured personnel carriers at close range.

After an intense 30-minute firefight, the area was secure, and Lindberg tallied up the damage. Two Pansarbandvagn 302 personnel carriers had been lost along with three Stridsvagn from the southern group. Overall Swedish casualties had been light. He ordered his men to prepare for the eventual counterattack.

As they began preparing their positions, he heard a sound that made his blood run cold – the low thumping drone of the rotors of Hind helicopters in the distance.

The other half of the new type 63 mechanised battalions are the *Pansarskyttekompanier* (armoured shooter/rifle companies). Each battalion had two companies with three *Pansarskyttepluton* (armoured shooter/rifle platoon) and a *Pansarvärnspluton* (anti-tank platoon). Additional weapons units from the battalion and brigade provided further anti-tank and armoured support.

Combat attacks carried out in slightly broken terrain with the armoured infantry companies were conducted with support provided by the battalion's tank companies. More open terrain attacks were conducted by the tank companies, with the armoured infantry being used for flank protection and follow-up clearing tasks.

When conducting an assault on enemy positions the *Pansarskyttepluton* trained for two different options; the *Kort stormning* (Brief Assault) or the *Uppsutten stormning* (Mounted Assault).

In a *Kort stormning* the armoured infantry is driven up in their Pbv 302 armoured carriers to the assault distance (the risk distance for splinters from their own artillery fire). The infantry then dismount and continue the attack on foot, supported by the weapons of their Pbv 302 armoured personnel carriers (APCs). A *Kort stormning* is used when it is not possible to drive past the assault distance due to the risk of having a carrier with mounted personnel knocked out. This may be due to mines, other terrain obstacles, or a strong enemy defence.

In a *Uppsutten stormning*, the enemy is suppressed by high-explosive fire from artillery or tanks. The infantry passes the assault distance mounted, and the Pbv 302 APCs drive at top speed into the enemy's fighting positions. Then the supporting fire is moved to a new position and the battle is carried out from the vehicles' weapons ports, or, if the terrain or the enemy's actions force it, dismounted on foot. *Uppsutten stormning* occurs when the terrain allows it and the enemy's counterattack potential is judged to be low.

Combined arms attacks are also exercised in conjunction with the tanks. The tanks would advance in front of the armoured infantry (in the event of a *Kort stormning*) or in front of the Pbv 302 APCs. The smooth interaction on the move between the tank and armoured infantry elements was something that was constantly practiced.

SWEDISH PBV 302 ARMOURED RIFLE COMPANY

PBV 302 ARMOURED RIFLE COMPANY

SVENSKA ARMÉN

You must field the Formation HQ and one Combat Unit from each black box.
You may also field one Combat Unit from each grey box.

• INFANTRY FORMATION • HQ TRANSPORT •

PBV 302 ARMOURED RIFLE COMPANY HQ
TSV103

- 1x AK 4 rifle team
- 1x Pbv 302 (TSV105)

1 POINT

COURAGE 3+	SKILL 2+
MORALE 3+	ASSAULT 4+
RALLY 3+	COUNTERATTACK 3+

IS HIT ON	INFANTRY SAVE
4+	3+

TACTICAL	TERRAIN DASH	CROSS COUNTRY DASH	ROAD DASH	CROSS
8"/20CM	8"/20CM	12"/30CM	12"/30CM	AUTO

WEAPON	RANGE	ROF HALTED	ROF MOVING	ANTI-TANK	FIRE-POWER	NOTES
AK 4 rifle team	16"/40CM	1	1	2	6	

INFANTRY
PBV 302 ARMOURED RIFLE PLATOON
TSV104 — 49

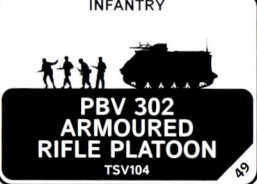

INFANTRY
PBV 302 ARMOURED RIFLE PLATOON
TSV104 — 49

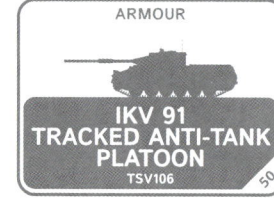

ARMOUR
IKV 91 TRACKED ANTI-TANK PLATOON
TSV106 — 50

ANTI-TANK
PVRBV 551 ANTI-TANK MISSILE PLATOON
TSV110 — 50

PVPJTGB RBS ANTI-TANK MISSILE PLATOON
TSV116 — 51

INFANTRY
PBV 302 ARMOURED RIFLE PLATOON
TSV104 — 49

ARMOUR
STRV 103 S-TANK TANK PLATOON
TSV102 — 43

STRV 104 CENTURION TANK PLATOON
TSV108 — 45

RECONNAISSANCE
PBV 302 ARMOURED RECON PLATOON
TSV114 — 51

ANTI-TANK
PVPJTGB 90MM ANTI-TANK PLATOON
TSV115 — 51

You may field a Combat Unit from a black box as a Support Unit for your Force.

SVENSKA ARMÉN
PBV 302 ARMOURED RIFLE PLATOON

PBV 302 ARMOURED RIFLE PLATOON	
3x Ksp-58 MG team with P-skott m/68 anti-tank	
3x Grg m/48 anti-tank team	
3x Pbv 302 (TSV105)	**7 POINTS**
2x Ksp-58 MG team with P-skott m/68 anti-tank	
2x Grg m/48 anti-tank team	
2x Pbv 302 (TSV105)	**4 POINTS**

OPTIONS
- Replace all P-skott m/68 anti-tank weapons with P-skott m/86 anti-tank weapons for +1 point for the Unit.
- Replace one Grg m/48 anti-tank team with RBS-56 BILL missile team for +1 point.

• INFANTRY UNIT •

COURAGE 4+	SKILL 3+
MORALE 4+	ASSAULT 4+
RALLY 4+	COUNTERATTACK 4+

IS HIT ON	INFANTRY SAVE
4+	3+

TACTICAL	TERRAIN DASH	CROSS COUNTRY DASH	ROAD DASH	CROSS
8"/20CM	8"/20CM	12"/30CM	12"/30CM	AUTO

WEAPON	RANGE	ROF HALTED	ROF MOVING	ANTI-TANK	FIRE-POWER	NOTES
Ksp-58 MG team or	16"/40CM	3	2	2	6	
P-skott m/68 anti-tank	12"/30CM	1	1	13	5+	HEAT, Slow Firing
OPTIONAL P-skott m/86 anti-tank	16"/40CM	1	1	17	5+	HEAT, Slow Firing
Grg m/48 anti-tank team	16"/40CM	1	1	17	3+	HEAT, Slow Firing
OPTIONAL RBS-56 BILL missile team	8"/20CM– 40"/100CM	1	-	22	3+	Assault 5, Guided, HEAT, Thermal Imaging

The Swedish *Pansarskyttepluton* (armoured rifle platoon) consists of a command group; three *skyttegrupper* (shooting groups); as well as a *granatgevärsgrupp* (grenade launcher group). A *skyttegrupp* consists of eight men. The *granatgevärsgrupp* are armed with three *Granatgevär m/48*, (Grg m/48 – "grenade rifle", model 1948, the 84mm Carl Gustav recoilless rifle).

Each *Skyttegrupp* is usually assigned four P-skott m/68 (74mm Miniman) disposible anti-tank weapons. Some units have been issued the new P-skott m/86 (84mm AT-4) anti-tank weapon. These are distributed so that within the group there are both anti-tank soldiers and AK4 (Swedish produced G3) riflemen, as well as the Ksp-58 (Swedish produced FN-MAG) machine-gun team.

The platoon Pansarbandvagn 302 (Pbv 302) is a high-mobility armoured personnel carrier built to Swedish requirements. The Pbv 302 has wide tracks and a high power-to-weight ratio, and has exceptionally good off-road mobility, and the low ground pressure enables it to operate over summer bog and winter snow. It is armed with the 20mm *automatkanon* (a licence built version of the French Hispano-Suiza type 804) fitted in a one-man turret on the left side of hull roof. It carries an infantry squad which is able to fight through two large roof hatches, though standard procedure would be to dismount through the two side-hinged doors at the rear of the Pbv 302 to fight.

SVENSKA ARMÉN
PBV 302 TRANSPORT

• TANK ATTACHMENT • AMPHIBIOUS • PASSENGERS 2 •

COURAGE 4+	SKILL 3+
MORALE 4+	ASSAULT 5+
REMOUNT 4+	COUNTERATTACK 5+

IS HIT ON 4+		
FRONT	SIDE	TOP
3	2	1

TACTICAL	TERRAIN DASH	CROSS COUNTRY DASH	ROAD DASH	CROSS
10"/25CM	16"/40CM	24"/60CM	32"/80CM	3+

WEAPON	RANGE	ROF HALTED	ROF MOVING	ANTI-TANK	FIRE-POWER	NOTES
20mm m/47 autocannon	20"/50CM	3	2	6	5+	Anti-helicopter
7.62mm MG	16"/40CM	3	3	2	6	

Crew: 3 - commander, gunner, driver + 8 passengers
Weight: 14 tonnes
Length: 5.35m (17'6.6")
Width: 2.86m (9'4.6")
Height: 2.50m (8'2.4")
Armour: max. 23mm
Weapons: 20mm automatkanon m/47D 1x 7.62mm Ksp 58 MG
Speed: 66 km/h (41 mph)
Engine: Diesel, Volvo THD 100 270 hp (201 kW)
Range: 300 km (186 miles)

RBS-56 BILL

The RBS-56 BILL (Bofors Infantry, Light and Lethal) began development in 1979, was demonstrated in 1982, and entered field trials with the Swedish Army in 1985.

The RBS-56 BILL guided missile flies 75cm above the target axis and detonates over the target when triggered by a laser proximity fuse. The shaped charge warhead is fitted in the missile fuselage inclined at a 30° angle downwards to hit the target from above. With this top-attack profile, the shaped charge warhead hits a main battle tank's front armour at a reduced angle.

SVENSKA ARMÉN
IKV 91 TRACKED ANTI-TANK PLATOON

IKV 91 TRACKED ANTI-TANK PLATOON	
3x Ikv 91	**5 POINTS**

The *Infanterikanonvagn 91* (infantry cannon wagon 91, Ikv 91) is a high mobility assault gun developed for the Swedish army. Its design employs common components with the Pbv 302 APC series. The 91 in the name designates the calibre of its gun (9cm) and that it is the first vehicle of its type in service (1). The Ikv 91 was assigned to the Swedish infantry brigades and the 10th Mechanised Brigade.

• TANK UNIT • AMPHIBIOUS • INFRA-RED (IR) •

COURAGE 4+	SKILL 3+
MORALE 4+	ASSAULT 4+
REMOUNT 4+	COUNTERATTACK 4+

IS HIT ON 4+

FRONT	SIDE	TOP
3	1	1

TACTICAL	TERRAIN DASH	CROSS COUNTRY DASH	ROAD DASH	CROSS
10"/25CM	16"/40CM	24"/60CM	32"/80CM	3+

WEAPON	RANGE	ROF HALTED	ROF MOVING	ANTI-TANK	FIRE-POWER	NOTES
9cm gun	36"/90CM	2	1	17	3+	HEAT, Laser Rangefinder
7.62mm AA MG	16"/40CM	3	3	2	6	
7.62mm MG	16"/40CM	1	1	2	6	

SVENSKA ARMÉN
PVRBV 551 ANTI-TANK MISSILE PLATOON

PVRBV 551 ANTI-TANK MISSILE PLATOON	
3x Pvrbv 551	**3 POINTS**

The *Pansarvärnsrobotbandvagn 551* (Pvrbv 551) is a tank-hunter mounting an Improved TOW anti-tank guided missile system. The Pvrbv 551 is converted from the old *Infanterikanonvagn 102/103* self-propelled guns. A new superstructure has been built on the old chassis with a new engine and transmission installed. The vehicle is operated by a crew of four, a commander and driver seated at the front, while the gunner and loader are located in the middle of the hull under two large roof hatches.

• TANK UNIT • THERMAL IMAGING •

COURAGE 4+	SKILL 3+
MORALE 4+	ASSAULT 5+
REMOUNT 4+	COUNTERATTACK 5+

IS HIT ON 4+

FRONT	SIDE	TOP
3	1	0

TACTICAL	TERRAIN DASH	CROSS COUNTRY DASH	ROAD DASH	CROSS
10"/25CM	14"/35CM	18"/45CM	24"/60CM	3+

WEAPON	RANGE	ROF HALTED	ROF MOVING	ANTI-TANK	FIRE-POWER	NOTES
Improved TOW missile	8"/20CM - 48"/120CM	1	-	21	3+	Guided, HEAT
7.62mm AA MG	16"/40CM	3	3	2	6	

When the Pvrbv 551 goes into firing position, the hatches are opened, the iTOW is raised above the vehicle roof, and the gunner and loader fire from an exposed position. In addition to the iTOW missile, the vehicle is also armed with a Ksp 58 machine-gun for self-defence.

SVENSKA ARMÉN
PBV 302 ARMOURED RECON PLATOON

PBV 302 ARMOURED RECON PLATOON	
3x Pbv 302 Scout	3 POINTS
2x Pbv 302 Scout	2 POINTS

The Pbv 302 *Pansarspaningspluton* (armoured reconnaissance platoon) provides the company with its eyes and ears, advancing ahead of the formation to discover the intentions and positions of the enemy. They are to find and report enemy activities, but not to engage.

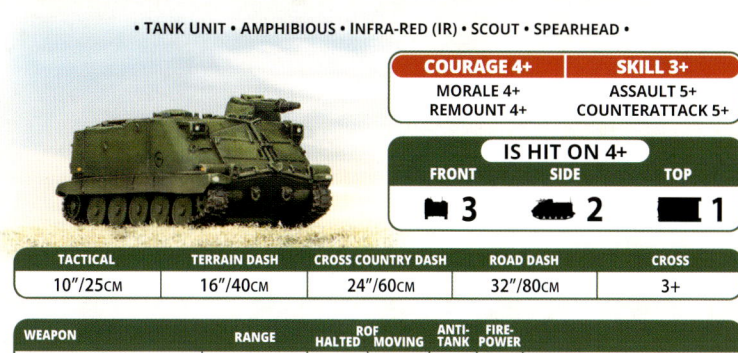

• TANK UNIT • AMPHIBIOUS • INFRA-RED (IR) • SCOUT • SPEARHEAD •

COURAGE 4+		SKILL 3+	
MORALE 4+		ASSAULT 5+	
REMOUNT 4+		COUNTERATTACK 5+	

IS HIT ON 4+		
FRONT	SIDE	TOP
3	2	1

TACTICAL	TERRAIN DASH	CROSS COUNTRY DASH	ROAD DASH	CROSS
10"/25CM	16"/40CM	24"/60CM	32"/80CM	3+

WEAPON	RANGE	ROF HALTED	ROF MOVING	ANTI-TANK	FIRE-POWER	
20mm m/47 autocannon	20"/50CM	3	2	6	5+	Anti-helicopter
7.62mm MG	16"/40CM	1	1	2	6	

SVENSKA ARMÉN
PVPJTGB RBS ANTI-TANK MISSILE PLATOON

PVPJTGB RBS ANTI-TANK MISSILE PLATOON	
3x Pvpjtgb RBS-55	4 POINTS
2x Pvpjtgb RBS-55	3 POINTS
3x Pvpjtgb RBS-56	4 POINTS
2x Pvpjtgb RBS-56	3 POINTS

The Volvo *Tgb 11* (Volvo C303) off-road vehicle was used as an anti-tank weapons platform for the RBS-55 iTOW and RBS-56 BILL anti-tank guided missile systems. It allowed the relatively large and cumbersome TOW or RBS-56 firing post to be moved and relocated easily, ideal in the defensive ambushing role expected of these weapons.

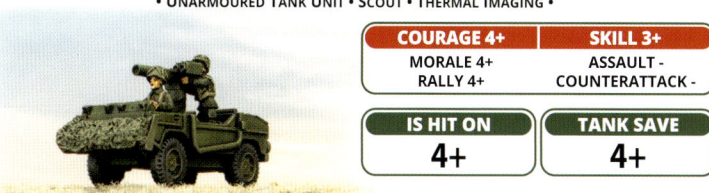

• UNARMOURED TANK UNIT • SCOUT • THERMAL IMAGING •

COURAGE 4+	SKILL 3+
MORALE 4+	ASSAULT -
RALLY 4+	COUNTERATTACK -

IS HIT ON	TANK SAVE
4+	4+

TACTICAL	TERRAIN DASH	CROSS COUNTRY DASH	ROAD DASH	CROSS
10"/25CM	12"/30CM	20"/50CM	48"/120CM	4+

WEAPON	RANGE	ROF HALTED	ROF MOVING	ANTI-TANK	FIRE-POWER	NOTES
RBS-55 (iTOW) missile	8"/20CM - 48"/120CM	1	-	21	3+	Guided, HEAT
RBS-56 BILL missile	8"/20CM - 40"/100CM	1	-	22	3+	Guided, HEAT

SVENSKA ARMÉN
PVPJTGB 90MM ANTI-TANK PLATOON

PVPJTGB 90MM ANTI-TANK PLATOON	
4x Pvpjtgb 90mm	4 POINTS
2x Pvpjtgb 90mm	2 POINTS

Pansarvärnspjästerrängbil 1111 (Pvpjtgb, armoured defence patrol car) was built by Volvo to suit the requirements of the Swedish army for a new all-terrain light utility vehicle. The resulting vehicle was the Volvo C303 the successor to the successful Volvo 903 Laplander, popularly known as "The Puppy". The original 903 beat out contenders from Willys, Land-Rover and Porsche, and became a long-serving member of the Swedish army.

It was built in many versions, such as troop carrier, radio car, fire truck, anti-tank missile launcher, and as a carrier for the *Pvpj 1110* Bofors 90mm recoilless anti-tank gun. As the conventional Puppy ran the risk of catching fire from the recoil flame of the 90mm recoilless gun, a special, low-profile body was developed by Volvo which made the vehicle look sportier than it was, and thus invited drivers to dangerous speeds. After a few accidents, a foldable rollbar was added.

• UNARMOURED TANK UNIT • SCOUT •

COURAGE 4+	SKILL 3+
MORALE 4+	ASSAULT -
RALLY 4+	COUNTERATTACK -

IS HIT ON	TANK SAVE
4+	4+

TACTICAL	TERRAIN DASH	CROSS COUNTRY DASH	ROAD DASH	CROSS
10"/25CM	12"/30CM	20"/50CM	48"/120CM	4+

WEAPON	RANGE	ROF HALTED	ROF MOVING	ANTI-TANK	FIRE-POWER	NOTES
90mm recoilless rifle	28"/70CM	2	1	17	3+	Accurate, HEAT, Recoilless

SWEDISH SUPPORT UNITS

SVENSKA ARMÉN
BANDKANON 1 ARMOURED HOWITZER BATTERY

BANDKANON 1 ARMOURED HOWITZER BATTERY	
3x Bandkanon 1	**9 POINTS**

The *Bandkanon 1*, (meaning 'tracked cannon 1'), is the primary Swedish self-propelled 155mm cannon. Its chassis was based on a lengthened Stridsvagn 103 S-Tank with one extra road wheel and armed with the Bofors 155mm L/60 automatic-cannon. This weapon has an exceptionally high rate of fire, being able to fire 14 shells in less than 45 seconds. With one round already loaded in the gun beside the two seven-round clips in the magazine. The magazine could then be reloaded with a built-in hoist in about two minutes.

• TANK UNIT •

COURAGE 4+	SKILL 3+
MORALE 4+	ASSAULT 5+
REMOUNT 4+	COUNTERATTACK 5+

IS HIT ON 4+
FRONT 2 | SIDE 1 | TOP 1

TACTICAL	TERRAIN DASH	CROSS COUNTRY DASH	ROAD DASH	CROSS
10"/25cm	12"/30cm	14"/35cm	16"/40cm	3+

WEAPON	RANGE	ROF HALTED	ROF MOVING	ANTI-TANK	FIRE-POWER	NOTES
15.5cm Kanon M/60	104"/260cm	ARTILLERY		4	2+	Autoloader, Forward Firing, Smoke Bombardment
or Direct fire	32"/80cm	1	1	18	1+	Brutal, Forward Firing, Slow Firing, Smoke
7.62mm AA MG	16"/40cm	3	3	2	6	

SVENSKA ARMÉN
EPBV 3022 FORWARD OBSERVER

EPBV 3022 FORWARD OBSERVER	
1x Epbv 3022 OP	**1 POINT**

You must field:
- a Bandkanon 1 Armoured Howitzer Battery (TSV112)

before you may field a Epbv 3022 Forward Observer.

The *Eldledningspansarbandvagn 3022* (Fire Control Tracked Vehcile, Epbv 3022) forward observer vehicle provides artillery observers and fire control personnel armoured protection as well as the equipment with which to find targets and direct the artillery on to them.

• INDEPENDENT TANK UNIT • AMPHIBIOUS • OBSERVER • SCOUT • THERMAL IMAGING •

COURAGE 4+	SKILL 3+
MORALE 4+	ASSAULT 5+
REMOUNT 4+	COUNTERATTACK 5+

IS HIT ON 4+
FRONT 3 | SIDE 2 | TOP 1

TACTICAL	TERRAIN DASH	CROSS COUNTRY DASH	ROAD DASH	CROSS
10"/25cm	16"/40cm	24"/60cm	32"/80cm	3+

WEAPON	RANGE	ROF HALTED	ROF MOVING	ANTI-TANK	FIRE-POWER	NOTES
20mm m/47 autocannon	20"/50cm	3	2	6	5+	Anti-helicopter
7.62mm MG	16"/40cm	3	3	2	6	

SVENSKA ARMÉN
LVRBV 701
ANTI-AIRCRAFT MISSILE PLATOON

LVRBV 701 ANTI-AIRCRAFT MISSILE PLATOON
3x Lvrbv 701 — **4 POINTS**

The *Luftvärnsrobotvagn 701* (Lvrbv 701) is based on the same conversion of the old *Infanterikanonvagn 103* self-propelled guns as the *Pansarvärnsrobotbandvagn 551* RBS 55 (TOW) ATGM carrier. The Lvrbv 701 self-propelled anti-aircraft vehicle is armed with the short range RBS 70 surface-to-air missile system.

• TANK UNIT • THERMAL IMAGING •

COURAGE 4+	SKILL 3+
MORALE 4+	ASSAULT 5+
REMOUNT 4+	COUNTERATTACK 5+

IS HIT ON 4+

FRONT	SIDE	TOP
3	1	0

TACTICAL	TERRAIN DASH	CROSS COUNTRY DASH	ROAD DASH	CROSS
10"/25CM	14"/35CM	18"/45CM	24"/60CM	3+

WEAPON	RANGE	ROF HALTED	ROF MOVING	ANTI-TANK	FIRE-POWER	
RBS 70 AA missile	56"/140CM	2	-	-	4+	Guided AA
7.62mm AA MG	16"/40CM	3	3	2	6	

SVENSKA ARMÉN
HKP 9 HELICOPTER PLATOON

HKP 9 HELICOPTER PLATOON
4x HKP 9 — **12 POINTS**
2x HKP 9 — **6 POINTS**

The HKP 9 is the West German Bo-105 helicopter purchased by Sweden to provide the army with a modern anti-tank helicopter. Rather than being armed with HOT missiles like the German variant, the HKP 9 is armed with the RBS 55 (iTOW) missile system. Each HKP 9 is armed with four missiles. The sight and guidance system for the missile, the HELITOW, were developed by the Swedish company SAAB.

• HELICOPTER UNIT • HUNTER-KILLER • THERMAL IMAGING •

COURAGE 4+	SKILL 3+
MORALE 4+	

IS HIT ON	AIRCRAFT SAVE
4+	5+

TACTICAL	TERRAIN DASH	CROSS COUNTRY DASH	ROAD DASH	CROSS
UNLIMITED				AUTO

WEAPON	RANGE	ROF HALTED	ROF MOVING	ANTI-TANK	FIRE-POWER	
Improved TOW missile	8"/20CM - 48"/120CM	1	-	21	3+	Guided, HEAT

Flights in wartime conditions were made at only 0-5 metres above the ground, under bridges and power lines, to avoid discovery. The crew consisted of one pilot and one gunner.

SVENSKA FLYGVAPNET
VIGGEN ATTACK GROUP

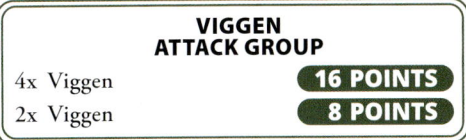

VIGGEN ATTACK GROUP
4x Viggen — **16 POINTS**
2x Viggen — **8 POINTS**

The Saab 37 Viggen (Swedish for Thunderbolt) is a Swedish single-seat, single-engine, short-medium range combat aircraft. It was used as an fighter, for ground attack, and reconnaissance. It was designed with a radical canard and delta wing configuration. The Viggen entered service in 1971. It was the first canard (the little wings at the front) design produced in quantity and was also one the most advanced fighter jets produced in Europe until the arrival of the Tornado.

• STRIKE AIRCRAFT UNIT •

COURAGE 4+	SKILL 3+
MORALE 4+	

IS HIT ON	AIRCRAFT SAVE
4+	5+

TACTICAL	TERRAIN DASH	CROSS COUNTRY DASH	ROAD DASH	CROSS
UNLIMITED				AUTO

WEAPON	RANGE	ROF HALTED	ROF MOVING	ANTI-TANK	FIRE-POWER	
Maverick missile	8"/20CM - 36"/90CM	-	1	27	2+	Brutal, Guided, HEAT
135mm rocket launcher	16"/40CM	SALVO		5	3+	One Shot
30mm cannon	8"/20CM	-	2	7	5+	Anti-helicopter

The AJ 37 Viggen strike fighter variant was designed to carry anti-ship missiles, AGM-65 Maverick (Swedish RB 75) television-guided missiles and unguided 135mm rockets in pods. The AJ 37 was also armed with a 30mm Oerlikon KCA cannon with 125 rounds.

SWEDISH SUPPORT UNITS

SWEDISH BASING & PAINTING

BASING SWEDISH INFANTRY

Formation Command AK 4 rifle team
Base the Commander on a small base with a radio operator and rifleman.

RBS-56 BILL missile team
Base RBS-56 BILL missile teams on a small base with a gunner and an assistant.

Grg m/48 anti-tank team
Base Grg m/48 anti-tank teams on a medium base. Teams combine a Grg m/48 anti-tank gunner and three riflemen.

Ksp-58 MG team with P-skott m/68 anti-tank

Ksp-58 MG team with P-skott m/86 anti-tank

Base Swedish Infantry teams team on a medium base. Teams combine a machine-gunner armed with a light machine-gun and riflemen armed with rifles and light anti-tank weapons (either P-skott m/68s or P-skott m/86s). Unit Leaders replace the machine-gun and a rifleman with an officer and radio operator.

SWEDISH VEHICLES

- LUFTWAFFE CAM. GREEN 823
- MEDIUM OLIVE 850
- LUFTWAFFE CAM. GREEN 823
- BEIGE BROWN 875
- BLACK GREY 862

Swedish Infantry

Flesh
Flat Flesh (955)

Beige Brown (875)

Rifles
Black Grey (862)

Webbing
German Field Grey (830)

Uniform
Uniform Green (922)

Pistol Pouch and Rifle Strap
Beige Brown (875)

Painted Metal
Olive Drab (887)

Boots
Ger. Cam. Black Brown (822)

Black 950

Luftwaffe Uniform 816

Olive Drab 887

Pale Blue 906

SWEDISH BASING & PAINTING

55

SWEDISH CATALOGUE

The following pages contain a catalogue of all the miniatures that are available to a Swedish force.

Swedish forces use products from the following nations catalogues:

🇸🇪 SWEDISH    WEST GERMAN

TNA950

FINNISH SWEDISH NORWEGIAN DANISH

Nordic Forces Decals

SWEDISH UNIT CARD PACK

🇸🇪 **Swedish Unit Cards** **WW3-08S**

CONTAINS: 18x Swedish Unit Cards, and 8x Finnish Allied Support Unit Cards.

TSWBX01

 ALL PLASTIC

CONTAINS:
3x Strv 103 S-Tanks

🇸🇪 **SWEDISH** **Strv 103 S-Tank Platoon**

TSWBX04

CONTAINS:
3x Ikv 91 Tanks

🇸🇪 **SWEDISH** **Ikv 91 Anti-tank Platoon**

56

TSWBX02

CONTAINS:
5x Strv 104 Centurion tanks

SWEDISH — Centurion Tank Platoon

TSWBX06

CONTAINS:
3x Bandkanon 1 Self-propelled Guns

SWEDISH — Bandkanon 1 Armoured Howitzer Battery

TSW120

RBS-55 (iTOW)

90mm Recoilless Rifle

CONTAINS:
4x Pvpjtgb 90mm Recoilless Rifle Jeeps,
Pvpjtgb RBS-55 (iTOW) Anti-tank Missile Jeeps, or
Pvpjtgb RBS-56 (BILL) Anti-tank Missile Jeeps

SWEDISH — Pvpjtgb 1111 Platoon

TSW702

Swedish Armoured Rifle Platoons have multiple different portable anti-tank rockets.

The P-skott m/86 is an upgrade option for the P-skott m/68, while the Grg m/48 is its own team type.

P-skott m/68   P-skott m/86   Grg m/48

CONTAINS:
- 1x AK 4 Rifle Team
- 3x Ksp-58 MG Team with P-skott m/68, or Ksp-58 MG Team with P-skott m/86
- 3x Grg m/48 Anti-tank Team
- 1x RBS-56 BILL Missile Team

SWEDISH — Armoured Rifle Platoon

TSWBX03

CONTAINS:
- 4x Pbv 302 Transports or Scouts, and
- 1x Optional turret for Epbv 3022 OP

SWEDISH — PBV 302 Platoon

TSWBX05

CONTAINS:
- 3x Pvrbv 551 TOW Carriers, or Lvrbv 701 SAM Carriers

SWEDISH — Pvrbv 551 or Lvrbv 701 Platoon

TSWSO02

Gunner's sight
iTOW missile pods

This product contains options to upgrade the HOT missiles of the West German BO-105 helicopters to iTOW missiles, and contains enough to upgrade two helicopters.

CONTAINS:
4x HKP 9 Missile Launchers
2x Gunner's Sights

SWEDISH — HKP 9 Missile Launchers (Direct Only)

TGBX12

ALL PLASTIC

CONTAINS:
2x Plastic BO-105P Helicopters
2x Plastic Flight Stands
8x Rare-earth Magnets

WEST GERMAN — PAH Anti-tank Helicopter Flight

TSWBX07

CONTAINS:
2x AJ 37 Viggen Attack Group

SWEDISH — AJ 37 Viggen Attack Group

NORWEGIAN

FORCES IN WORLD WAR III

WORLD WAR II

During World War II Norway was invaded by Germany due to its strategic location in the North Atlantic and its natural resources. Norway had declared itself neutral at the outbreak of war in 1939, but was still attacked by Germany in 1940. Later, Norway's strategic importance grew due to its closeness to the Allies' North Atlantic shipping convoy routes from the United States to the ice-free northern Soviet harbours along the Barents Sea coast, including the major port of Murmansk.

The Norwegians attempted to resist the German invaders, their most notable success being the sinking of the German battlecruiser Blücher in Oslo Fjord by the defences of the coastal artillery fortress Oscarsborg. However, Norway's small army was outclassed by the Germans. The Germans occupied the country and most regular resistance was abandoned a few months after the occupation.

THE COLD WAR

Norway had become sceptical of neutrality following the German occupation during World War II and the Soviet occupation of the Eastern European countries after the war. A Soviet invasion of Norway was regarded as possible. Norway was therefore one of the initial signatory parties to the treaty that formed NATO in 1949.

After the war, the Soviets developed the Kola Peninsula as one of the most comprehensive and highly fortified military centres in the world. Norway's almost 200 km border with Soviet Union was very close to the Kola Peninsula. The ice-free military harbours housed the Soviet Northern Fleet, with seven naval bases, several shipyards, air bases, and factories producing military equipment. The area was home to more than 200 submarines, most of them armed with nuclear weapons. Around two-thirds of all the Soviet Navy's nuclear force was based in the Kola Peninsula.

The main sea route from the Kola Peninsula to the Atlantic Sea was along the Norwegian coast. It formed the access route to the coastal areas of the United States and the Western European countries, as well as the American supply line to Europe in case of war. Northern Norway in particular thus became a cornerstone in the NATO defence system and this resulted in close military cooperation between the United States and Norway.

Northern Norway was developed as the first Western line of defence in case of war with the Soviet Union, and the whole of Norwegian society was prepared for a total defensive war in case of a Soviet invasion.

Behind this development was massive US economic support for the construction of air bases, harbours, arms reserves, fortifications, and monitoring and warning systems, as well as support for fully modernised Norwegian military forces, as well as comprehensive NATO intelligence service activities operated from Norway.

THE NORWEGIAN ARMY

Brigaden i Nord-Norge (Brigade in Northern Norway) was the Norwegian Army's main standing regular formation and in the event of war would be deployed immediately to the Finnmark border area. *Brigade i Sør-Norge* (Brigade in Southern Norway) and *12. Brigade* (12th Brigade) were also mechanised, but were formed from reservists.

The remaining nine brigades, each numbered after their defence district, were all Infantry Brigades, formed mainly from reservists, with a cadre of regulars.

The 17 defence districts varied widely in size and composition: many had no Regular or Reserve units at all, but simply provided command to the *Heimevernet* (Home Guard, or HV).

The *Heimevernet* was not the same as the Army Reserve. When Norwegians become 18 years old they are required to do national service for one year and were assigned to a *Heimevernet* district, each containing between five and ten platoons. With the outbreak of war, or earlier if there is enough warning, those eligible who had completed their training would be assigned to platoons for home defence duty. The *Heimevernet* was made up of 470 platoons with about a sixth of them assigned to anti-aircraft units.

Other Defence Districts (particularly in the Finnmark) included reserve and regular units such as infantry and artillery battalions, with which to back up the Home Guard. These units included three independent Armoured Squadrons. In war, it was proposed that three divisions would have been formed, but there were few permanent structures in place during peacetime and no permanently-assigned divisional support troops.

By the mid-1980s the Norwegian Army was structured to be able to grow from a peacetime force of 20,000 personnel to a fully mobilised strength of 160,000 troops in 13 brigades and dozens of independent units.

The Royal Norwegian Air Force (RNoAF) fielded approximately ninety combat aircraft, and the Royal Norwegian Navy (RNN) focused its efforts on countering amphibious landings, fielding a large number of small vessels designed to operate in local waters, as well as a network of coastal fortifications.

In the event of war NATO would provide Norway reinforcements consisting of the British 3rd Marine Commando Brigade (including a Dutch contingent), the US 4th Marine Expeditionary Brigade, and the multi-national Allied Mobile Force.

WORLD WAR III

During the Cold War, Norway held the dubious distinction of being one of only two NATO nations to share a border with the the Soviet Union.

With the likelihood of war growing it seemed Moscow's priorities in Norway centred on destroying or capturing Norwegian airfields to prevent them being utilised for offensive operations against military assets based in the nearby Kola Peninsula. This was combined with a planned offensive into northern Norway to secure these facilities for their own use. Once captured the Soviets could then use these as a base for offensive air and naval operations against NATO forces in the North Sea and North Atlantic.

NATO's Cold War plans to support Norway on land centred on early deployment of up to four brigades. The Allied Command Europe (ACE) Mobile Force (Land) acted as NATO's rapid reaction formation, and whilst in theory a 'go anywhere' force, it would probably have headed to Norway in a crisis. This would have been joined by the United Kingdom/Netherlands Amphibious Force, the Canadian Air-Sea Transportable Brigade Group (CAST) and the American Norway Air-Landed Marine Expeditionary Brigade. Around two hundred combat aircraft were assigned to support these units. In time, the US Marine deployment would likely have grown into a full 50,000-strong Marine Expeditionary Force.

Off the Norwegian coast, NATO's efforts are based around the US-led Maritime Strategy: multiple naval battle groups taking up defensive positions in Norway's fjords, before advancing to strike Soviet bases in the Kola Peninsula. Maritime control of the region was also vital in ensuring that NATO's Atlantic lines of communication were not successfully interdicted by the Soviet submarine fleet and air assets.

Though the tide of war broke over NATO on 4 August 1985, the divisions of the Soviet 6th Combined Arms Army did not cross the Norwegian and Finnish borders until 7 August 1985. The Norwegians, who were well aware of the Soviet build-up on their borders were on high alert.

In Norway's Finnmark region border guards and the advanced elements of the *Brigaden i Nord-Norge* conducted a fighting withdrawal westwards, laying ambushes along the main routes of the Soviet advance. However, Soviet air assault helicopter-borne and naval landing forces struck airbases, ports, and other military installations ahead of the advancing 54th Motor Rifle Division.

By the end of the first week of the conflict the Soviet 61st Independent Naval Landing Brigade had successfully taken Norway's Banak Air Station. This important airfield at the end of the Porsanger Fjord saw the Soviet naval troops overcome the troops defending the airport. The 54th Motor Rifle Division, and the following 16th Motor Rifle Division, after cutting through Finnish Lapland, had their advance slowed as they encountered the elite troops of the *Brigaden i Nord-Norge*, which was being reinforced by brigades arriving from southern Norway.

NATO reinforcements had begun to make their way to the front by the second week of the conflict in Norway. The British/Netherlands Commando Brigade had come ashore at Trondheim, but the US 2nd Marine Division was still being held back for their possible use in Denmark if required.

The Soviet air force had concentrated on targeting Norway's airports and seaports with bombing, though it had had to run the gauntlet of NATO, as well as Swedish and Finnish, fighter interception.

More Norwegian brigades had also begun to arrive in Finnmark, though the rapid advance of the Soviet forces had seen the focus of the Norwegian defence concentrated around the mountain passes in the west of Finnmark and the Frøy defensive positions.

In northern Finland the Finns and Swedes had formed a rough defensive line running along the Finno-Swedish border. The Soviets seemed content not to press too hard southwards, having achieved their passage into Norway.

As the third week of the war began the situation in Norway sees the Norwegians and their NATO allies holding the passes that lead into central Norway.

BRIGADEN I NORD-NORGE

"Raskere, løp," Sersjant Solberg encouraged his section to speedily dismount their NM135 transport.

They hurriedly bounded down the track's ramp and made their way up the slope toward the positions of the squadron. Solberg closely followed. Once in position he could see the Soviet infantry swarming down from the hills about 1500 metres away on the other side of the shallow river valley. They had dismounted and their tracked carriers followed some distance to the rear. Slightly ahead of the infantry were about 30 tanks, T-55s from their silhouettes Solberg guessed.

The NM135 vehicles had taken positions behind with their hulls obscured by the crest of the hill and their 20mm armed turrets sitting above the with a view of the approaching enemy. Solberg also knew there were some NM142 iTOW anti-tank tracks nearby.

As the Soviets began closing on Norwegian positions a burst of machine-gun fire struck out from the position of the first troop further down the slope. Several Soviet riflemen dropped to the ground. More machine-guns joined them from both first troop and second troop, who were positioned on the left.

A flash appeared from one of the T-55s behind the Soviet riflemen, quickly followed by an explosion of earth and saplings just in front of first troop's position. The first line of enemy tanks had halted and were peppering the Norwegian forward positions with high-explosive rounds.

A crack and whoosh off to the right alerted Solberg to the presence of the NM142 troop firing a iTOW missile. He watched the rear of the missile's rocket motor burning its way towards a T-55. It hit, creating a flash and a cloud of dust and smoke, before something ignited and the tank began to burn. More missile fire soon hammered into the Soviet tanks.

With the infantry now well within range, the NM135 tracks opened up with their 20mm cannons, joining the machine-guns targeting the Soviet riflemen. Solberg's troop commander signalled his section to join first and second troops' fire.

Solberg noted that a T-55 on the extreme left flank began burning, though it was not in the immediate fire zone of the NM142s. Then another went up. It seemed one of the battalion's Leopard 1 tank squadrons had arrived and taken a position on the flank.

With increasing numbers of tanks burning and the riflemen running into heavy fire, the Soviets were beginning to waver. Groups of riflemen began retiring towards their transports, which had begun to withdraw back up the slope on the other side of the valley.

"Keep up the fire until they are out of range," he spurred on his men, "we don't want them coming back!"

Brigaden i Nord-Norge (Brigade in Northern Norway, or Brig N) is the Norwegian Army's (*Hæren*) main standing regular formation. In the event of war it would be deployed immediately to the Finnmark border area on border containment. *Brigaden i Nord-Norge* was formed when the *Tysklandsbrigaden* (German Brigade, a Norwegian unit stationed in British occupied zone of West Germany) was withdrawn home to Norway. The brigade is a main component in Norway's immediate land defense against an invasion by the Soviet Union.

The *Storting* (Norway's national assembly) decided to establish two brigades in Norway, one in the south and one in the north.

Allied NATO military advisers recommended that Norway should organise their field army into three divisions, a 1st Division command in the east, a 3rd Division command in the south, and a 6th Division command in the north. Eventually only 1st and 6th Division commands were approved.

On 1 September 1953, the *Brigaden i Nord-Norge* was formally declared operational. The task of this new standing brigade was to be twofold: act as a standing contingency force in vulnerable areas until the country had mobilised its conscripted forces, and to provide first-time service conscripts with training and education.

The 6th Division command, parent command of the brigade, was established at Elvegårdsmoen, just north of Narvik.

With the outbreak of war, the northern Norway district command of the 6th Division would mobilise its reserve forces, *14. Brigade* and *15. Brigade*, to reinforce the regular *Brigaden i Nord-Norge*.

By the mid-1980s *Brigaden i Nord-Norge* consisted of its Headquarters, a Mechanised Reconnaissance Squadron, 1st Armoured Battalion, 2nd Infantry Battalion, 3rd Infantry Battalion, a self-propelled Field Artillery Battalion, a Mechanised Anti-tank Squadron, a Mechanised Anti-aircraft Company, and a Engineer Company.

GUNDERSEN'S STRIDSVOGNESKADRON

The weeks of July had begun with concern across the squadron. Had things really got so bad that some sort of peaceful resolution could not be arrived at? When the order to fully mobilise the Brigaden i Nord-Norge arrived in the third week of July all speculation was left behind. The men of the brigade set about readying their equipment, weapons, and vehicles and began deploying to their forward positions.

Rittmester Yngvar Gundersen's Leopard 1 Stridsvogneskadron was one of two tank squadrons, along with two mechanised infantry squadrons in the 1st Armoured Battalion. The brigade's role was to delay any Soviet advance across Finnmark for as long as possible through defence in depth using aggressive mobile action, ambushing, counterattacking and giving ground to slow the Soviet advance as required. This would buy time for both Norwegian and NATO reinforcements to arrive.

Unlike western and central Europe, Northern Norway was not criss-crossed with an extensive road network, nor made up of gentle farmland. In the summer Finnmark was mostly wild rocky tundra and pasture where the Sami grazed their reindeer. The tundra is broken up with patches of low scrub made up of mountain birch and other plants, providing some concealment. The coast is indented by large fjords. However, Finnmark is not as mountainous as other parts of Norway, especially its central and eastern areas. It is further broken up by rivers and lakes. Only one main east-west road runs from the Soviet border near Kirkenes along the Finnish border, before branching in central Finnmark to the north, northwest, and south. Other roads consist of secondary county roads that run to and along the northern coast. To travel by road to the southwestern part of Finnmark and the rest of Norway you must travel through Finland or Sweden to the south, or head northwest and take the coastal road.

This likely meant any Soviet attack across Finnmark would not entirely rely on the road network for its access or its axis of travel.

BATTLE GROUP

Gundersen's squadron and a mechanised infantry squadron from the battalion had been organised into a battle group. It was assigned the task of delaying the advance of the Soviets from the direction of Kirkenes. The advance was following the axis of the Tanafjord Road (Fylkesvei 98 (Fv98), County Road 98) that ran from Tana Bru in the east through Ifjord at the foot of the Laksefjorden, before eventually arriving at Lakselv on the Porsangerfjorden, just north of the Porsanger Army Garrison.

The border guards had withdrawn ahead of the Soviets crossing the border in the early hours of 7 August 1985. These lightly armed troops watched their movements, reporting the Soviets progress. By midmorning the border guards had withdrawn across the Tana River at Tana Bru. They reported the lead elements of the Soviet forces were at most an hour behind them.

Norwegian Army engineers had prepared the Tana Bru bridge crossing the Tana River for demolition. The next nearest crossing was 70 km to the southwest at the Utsjoki ferry on the Finnish border. The Norwegians knew that the Soviets were well-equipped with amphibious vehicles, but denying them the bridge would hinder the movement of their non-amphibious vehicles and force them to deploy bridging equipment. On the arrival of the last border guards at Tana Bru the engineers blew the bridge and headed north to their first delaying position near Rustefjelbma, in the high ground surrounding the road about 1.5 km west of Rustefjelbma.

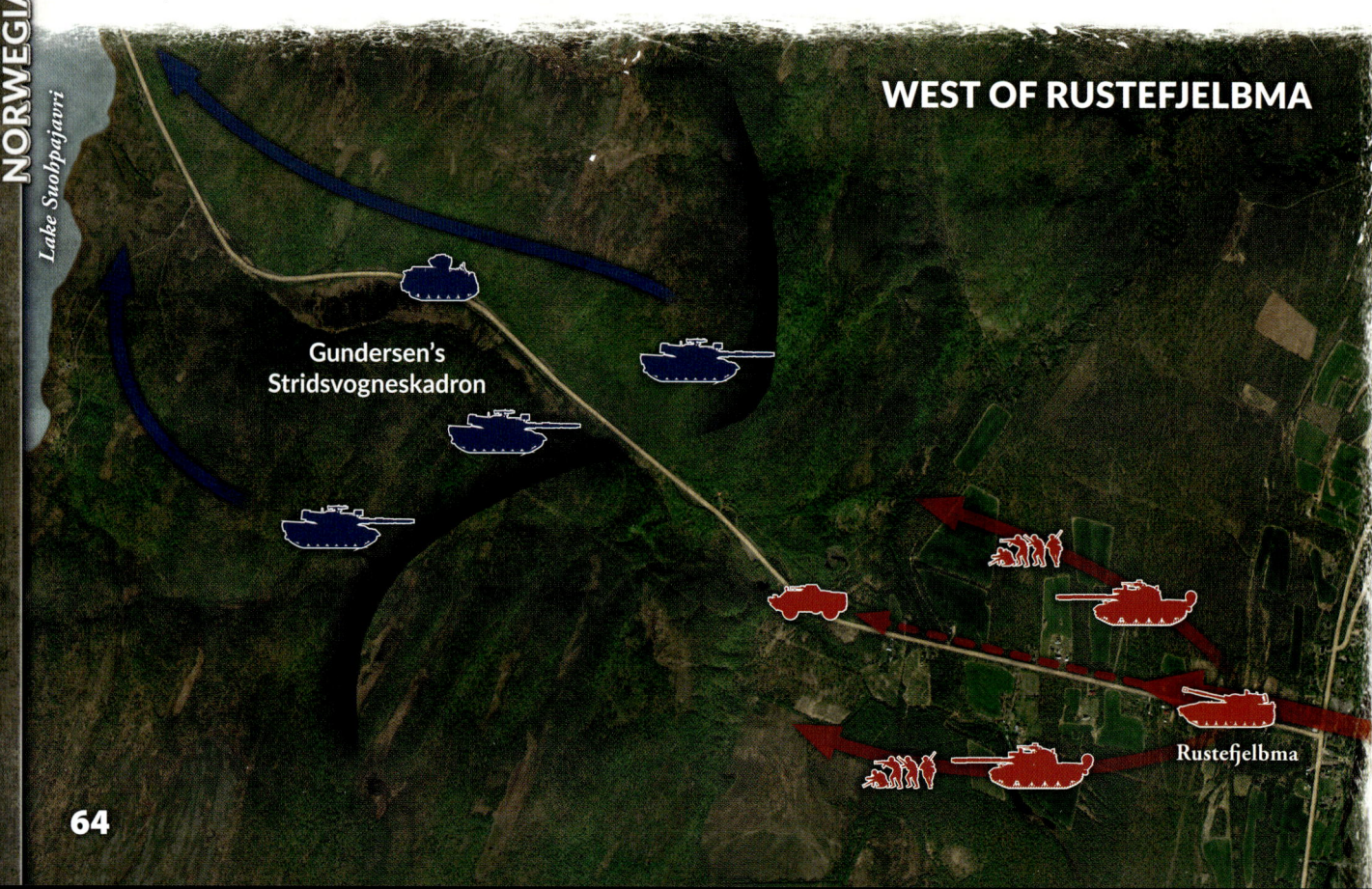

VESTERANA

WEST OF RUSTEFJELBMA

In the meantime, Gundersen had set up his tanks in two positions on either side of the road on the higher ground to overwatch the approach of any Soviet vehicles heading out of Rustefjelbma westwards on the Fv98 road. A troop of NM142 TOW missile vehicles had also taken up an overwatching position. The small trees and shrubs covering the hills and slopes provided good concealment, but were light enough to allow easy movement through.

On the evening of 7 August, the Soviets sent a probe out from Rustefjelbma. The lead Soviet recon vehicles were hit by fire from Gundersen's tanks as they travelled along the road towards the hills, leaving several burning wrecks strung out along the road. The Soviets immediately withdrew.

The Norwegians shifted positions further west along the road and not long after Soviet artillery dropped on their former positions. Later that night the Soviets mounted an attack through the hills on a much wider front. The Norwegians were forced to withdraw or risk being outflanked. They retired past Lake Suohpajavri during the early morning of 8 August and across country towards Vestertana before re-joining the Fv98 road westwards.

VESTERANA

Along the road between Vesterana and Ifjord a number of ambush positions were established, on the hillier terrain immediately west of Vesterana, and then again closer to Ifjord where the road is hemmed in by small lakes and hills.

The Soviets ran into the first ambush position about midday. Initially the NM142 anti-tank vehicles knocked out the leading tanks at long range, before a troop of Leopards joined in to knock out another three tanks. The Soviets halted and then withdrew back down the road and out of sight of the Norwegians. The Norwegian ambush group immediately withdrew several kilometres along the road to another position where they had a good view of a narrow gap that the Soviets would have to funnel through.

ROAD TO IFJORD

The Soviets were more cautious when they continued their advance later in the afternoon. Norwegian scouts posted to watch the road soon sent warning of the Soviets approach. This time only a few BMPs appeared along the road where it emerged around a hill. Not long after the NM142s opened fire on the exposed BMPs, destroying the leading vehicle, their shooting was interrupted by incoming fire from the high ground south of the road. One of the TOW tracks was hit and the crew were forced to bail out when it began to burn. The Soviets had moved a company of tanks off the road to the south and they had begun to fire on the Norwegian positions. One troop of Leopards engaged the tanks, identified as T-55s, while the rest of the ambush group withdrew and headed for their next positions further west.

Throughout the evening and into the night, Gundersen's battle group withdrew towards and through Ifjord, dogged by the recon elements of the Soviet division snapping at their heels. They arrived at their new positions in the early hours of 9 August. The defence of Finnmark was in full swing.

IFJORD

BRIGADE NORD
NORWEGIAN FORCE

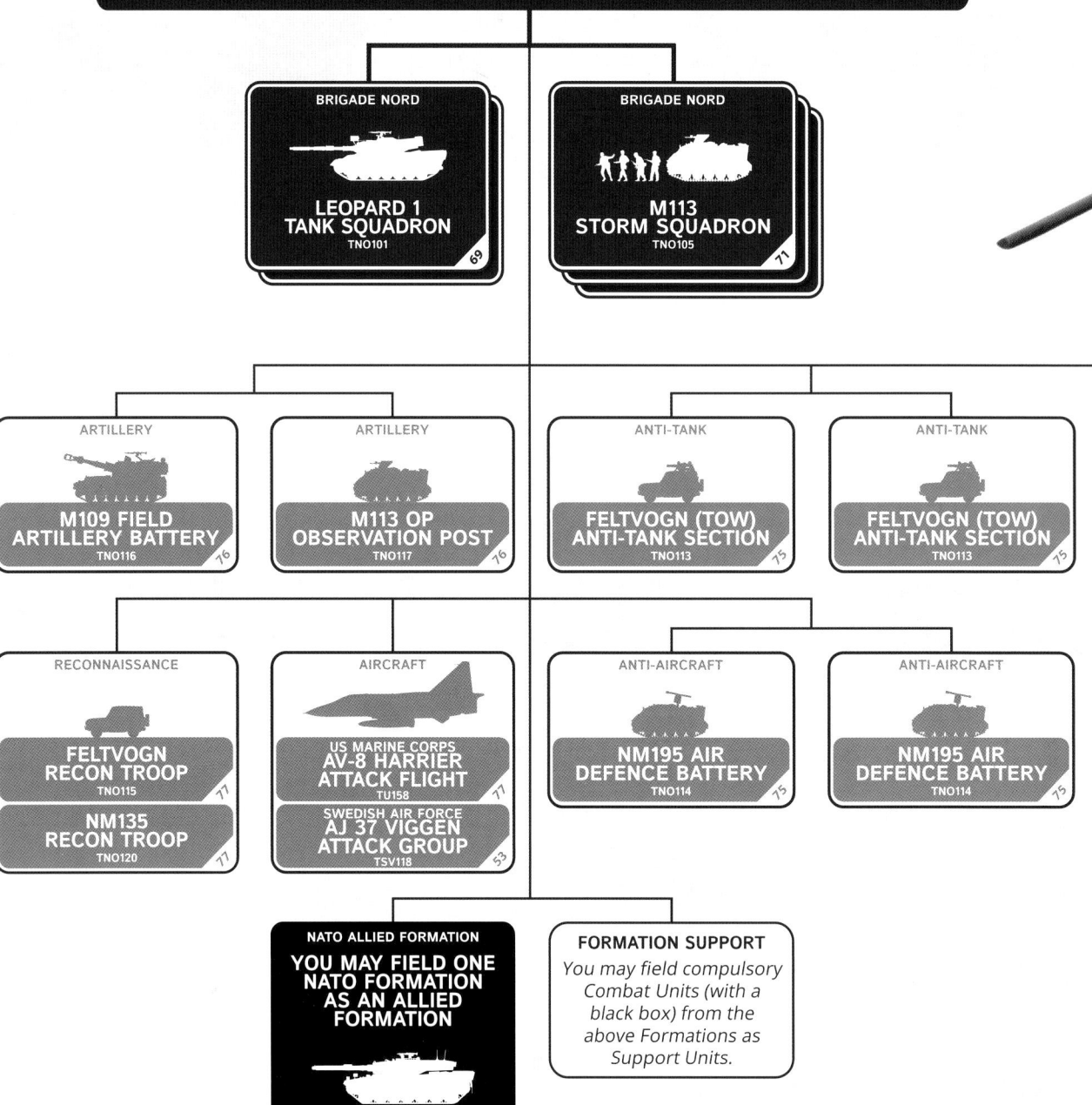

NORWEGIAN SPECIAL RULES

The Norwegian Army (*Hæren*) has a number of features and weapons. These are reflected in the following special rules.

BAZOOKA SKIRTS

Leopard 1 tanks are fitted with 'bazooka skirts', spaced armour to protect them from light, hand-held anti-tank weapons.

> Teams with Bazooka Skirts have Front and Side armour rating of 10 against HEAT weapons.

TOW-2 WEAPONS

The new TOW-2 anti-tank guided missile enlarged the warhead again over that of the Improved TOW missile.

> A number of Units have options to have TOW-2 missiles instead of Improved TOW missiles.
>
> If you take any units with TOW-2 missiles you must take ALL options with TOW-2 missiles in your Force.

US MARINE CORPS ALLIED SUPPORT

ARMOURED
M60 PATTON TANK PLATOON — TU142 — 71

ARTILLERY
MARINE M109 ARTILLERY BATTERY — TU156 — 80

ANTI-AIRCRAFT
HMMWV SAM PLATOON — TU130 — 63

AIRCRAFT
AH-64 APACHE ATTACK HELICOPTER PLATOON — TU172 — 60
AH-1 COBRA ATTACK HELICOPTER PLATOON — TU111a — 60

INFANTRY
RIFLE PLATOON — TU146 — 75

Rules for American Formations and Units are found in the pages marked in WWIII-03 World War III: American.

NATO ALLIED SUPPORT

A number of units from other NATO nations, such as the US Marine Corps brigades, have been assigned to reinforce Norway in case of war.

A NATO Allied Formation can be from any other Force with a NATO Allied Formation in its support.

You can take an Allied Formation or Units as part of your Force. An Allied Formation or Unit obeys all the rules for its own nationality. An Allied Formation Commander can only join Units in its own Formation or nationality and only its Formation or nationality Units can benefit from its Command Leadership (see page 25 and 64 of the rulebook).

An Allied Formation does not count as a Formation when counting how many Formations are left when determining if you have lost the game (see page 65 of the rulebook).

LEOPARD 1 TANK SQUADRON

It started raining just after noon, and an hour later Sersjant Kjell Jørgensen sat out of his Leopard 1 tank commander's cupola peering though his field glasses across the tundra, the water dripping from the hood of his parka. He was about to lean down and grab his thermos of coffee when a glint caught his eye. He brought his glasses up and adjusted the focus, bringing into view a Soviet BMP popping in and out of cover as it went up and down with the undulations of the ground.

"Arve, BMP, 2000 metres, confirm," Jørgensen called to his gunner though the tank's internal communication net.

"Got it, confirmed, 1950 metres and closing," Visekorporal Arve Dahl replied, "there seems to be a second vehicle immediately following," he paused for a few moments, "and a larger group, tanks I think, following another 400 metres behind."

"So it begins," Jørgensen muttered to himself, before he switched his radio to the troop channel to give his troop commander the good news. He quickly received the order to engage.

"Ignore the BMPs for the moment Arve, concentrate on those tanks," Sersjant Jørgensen instructed his gunner.

With a 105mm sabot round already in the breech, Dahl laid the gun to bear onto the approaching tanks. Now that they were a bit closer he was able to identify them as T-72s from their profile, even though the rain was not creating the ideal conditions for visibility. He waited for his target tank to hit a rise as it moved though the undulations.

"Away," Dahl signalled he has fired. "Sabot," he ordered up another round from his loader, Ole Pedersen.

"Hit! Nice," acknowledged Jørgensen, "another T-72 is about 25 metres to the right."

"Up," Pedersen confirmed the reload and tapped Dahl's shoulder. Another round quickly added to the destruction.

By this point the rest of the troop had joined in and several more enemy tanks were burning among the scrubby vegetation of the tundra.

At the end of World War II the Norwegians had to rebuild their military from scratch after their defeat and occupation by the Germans.

As part of support for their European allies, the United States supplied Norway with their first 17 M24 Chaffees in 1946. When Norway joined NATO in 1949 more Chaffees were supplied. The Chaffee gave the Norwegian Army their first experience operating a relatively modern armoured vehicle. Eventually, Norway would operate a total of 141 Chaffees and, through upgrades, keep them in service into the 1980s.

Being a member of NATO opened the way for the importation of further military equipment from its western allies.

In 1968, Norway ordered 172 Leopard 1 tanks for the Norwegian Cavalry, the army's mechanised component.

The Leopard 1 tanks were then allocated to the tank squadrons from Trøndelag northwards covering northern Norway. A full standing tank squadron was stationed at Bardufoss, a reduced tank squadron in Bodø, a squadron at Andøya, and a squadron at Porsangmoen. In the mid-1980s these independent tank squadrons were assembled into armoured battalions.

These new armoured battalions followed the Swedish example and were organised as mixed formations with two squadrons of tanks and two squadrons of mechanised infantry.

BRIGADE NORD
LEOPARD 1 TANK SQUADRON

You must field the Formation HQ and one Combat Unit from each black box.
You may also field one Combat Unit from each grey box.

LEOPARD 1 TANK SQUADRON HQ — TNO101

2x Leopard 1		**6 POINTS**
1x Leopard 1		**3 POINTS**

• TANK FORMATION • BAZOOKA SKIRTS • INFRA-RED (IR) •

COURAGE 3+	SKILL 2+
MORALE 3+	ASSAULT 4+
REMOUNT 3+	COUNTERATTACK 3+

IS HIT ON 4+

FRONT	SIDE	TOP
9	5	1

TACTICAL	TERRAIN DASH	CROSS COUNTRY DASH	ROAD DASH	CROSS
10"/25CM	18"/45CM	28"/70CM	32"/80CM	2+

WEAPON	RANGE	ROF HALTED	ROF MOVING	ANTI-TANK	FIRE-POWER	NOTES
105mm L7 gun	40"/100CM	2	2	19	2+	Laser Rangefinder, Smoke, Stabiliser
7.62mm AA MG	16"/40CM	3	3	2	6	
7.62mm MG	16"/40CM	1	1	2	6	

ARMOUR — LEOPARD 1 TANK TROOP (TNO102)
ARMOUR — LEOPARD 1 TANK TROOP (TNO102)
INFANTRY — M113 STORM TROOP (TNO106)
ANTI-TANK — NM142 ANTI-TANK TROOP (TNO111)
ARMOUR — LEOPARD 1 TANK TROOP (TNO102)
ARTILLERY — M106 107MM MORTAR TROOP (TNO110)

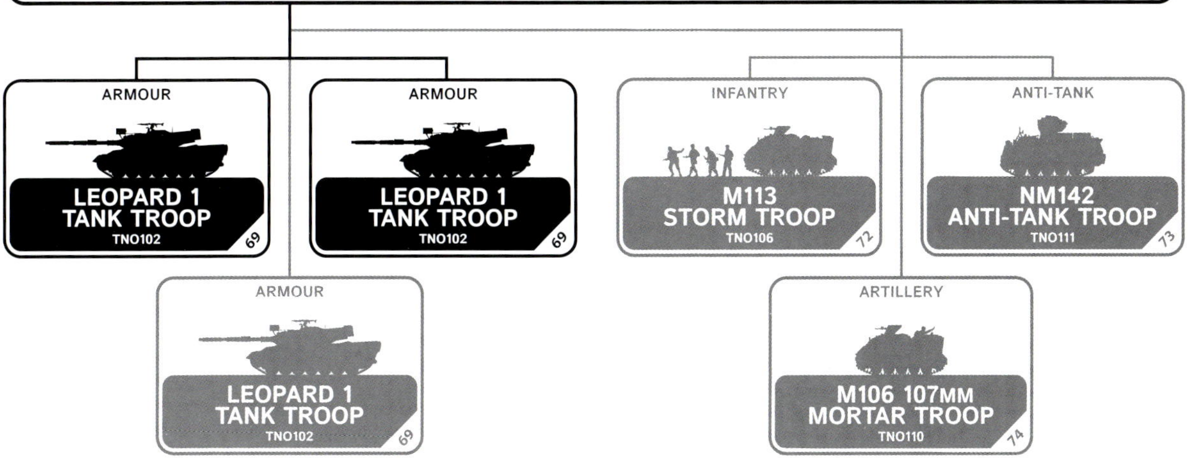

You may field a Combat Unit from a black box as a Support Unit for your Force.

BRIGADE NORD
LEOPARD 1 TANK TROOP

LEOPARD 1 TANK TROOP

4x Leopard 1		**12 POINTS**
3x Leopard 1		**9 POINTS**

• TANK UNIT • BAZOOKA SKIRTS • INFRA-RED (IR) •

COURAGE 4+	SKILL 3+
MORALE 4+	ASSAULT 4+
REMOUNT 3+	COUNTERATTACK 4+

IS HIT ON 4+

FRONT	SIDE	TOP
9	5	1

TACTICAL	TERRAIN DASH	CROSS COUNTRY DASH	ROAD DASH	CROSS
10"/25CM	18"/45CM	28"/70CM	32"/80CM	2+

WEAPON	RANGE	ROF HALTED	ROF MOVING	ANTI-TANK	FIRE-POWER	NOTES
105mm L7 gun	40"/100CM	2	2	19	2+	Laser Rangefinder, Smoke, Stabiliser
7.62mm AA MG	16"/40CM	3	3	2	6	
7.62mm MG	16"/40CM	1	1	2	6	

From 1970 Norway's front line tank was the Leopard 1. These were stationed in the north of the country where the most likely threat of Soviet attack would be directed.

Though not as heavily armoured as the Soviet tanks they potentially faced, the well-trained Norwegian crews combined with the excellent 105mm L7 gun give the Leopard 1 good odds against T-55 and T-62 tanks, and with the capability of taking on T-72s with good use of concealment and movement.

Crew: 4 - commander, gunner, loader, driver
Weight: 42.2 tonnes
Length: 9.54m (31' 3.5")
Width: 3.37m (11' 0.5")
Height: 2.7m (8' 10")
Armour: steel 19-21.7mm and 10-70 mm RHA
Weapons: 105mm Royal Ordnance L7A3 L/52 rifled gun
2x MG3 7.62mm MG
Speed: 65 km/h (46 mph)
Engine: MTU MB 838 CaM 500, 10-cylinder, multi-fuel engine, 819 hp (610 kW)
Range: 600 km (373 miles)

M113 STORM SQUADRON

The section had scrambled up the low rise to the edge of the low scrub that covered most of the area. From the east, along the road that wound around the edge of the high ground, a column of Soviet vehicles approached. Leading the advance was a group of T-55 tanks. Several hundred metres behind them followed a group of tracked vehicles, crowded with the hunched figures of Soviet riflemen perched on their backs. The report from the scouts had been accurate: the Soviets' recon had already passed, and this was the main body.

Grenader (Grenadier) Nils Ommundsen readied his Carl Gustav recoilless rifle, while Menig (Private) Ulf Karlsen withdrew a round from the carry case and pushed it into the back of the weapon sitting on Ommundsen's right shoulder. Further east along the ridge the troop's other two Carl Gustav teams readied their weapons.

Once the lead T-55 had passed Ommundsen's position, Løytnant Berg signalled the troop to fire. Ommundsen fired the Carl Gustav into the rear flank of the passing tank at about 75 metres. The round struck the tank and it was soon burning. The Soviet tank crew quickly decamped and scrambled over the side of the road to take cover from the incoming fire.

Further along the road, the Storm Squadron's fire had knocked out the trailing T-55, leaving the remaining five tanks stuck between the position of the Norwegians on the higher ground and the slope leading down to the valley below.

"Reload, HEAT," Ommundsen instructed Karlsen, "let's see if we can get another, Ulf!"

Karlsen shoved in another round and slapped Ommundsen on the helmet to indicate the reload.

Back down the road the Soviet riflemen were hastily dismounting from their tracks and began an erratic fire on the Stormtropp's position.

To the west, where the road curved around the next hill, a flash appeared at the crest of the hill. A few moments later the second T-55 in the leading group was hit with a bright flash as it attempted to push past its burning comrade. The squadron's NM142 TOW anti-tank vehicles had joined the ambush.

Ommundsen quickly adjusted his aiming point to the third T-55, and fired.

BRIGADE NORD
M113 STORM SQUADRON

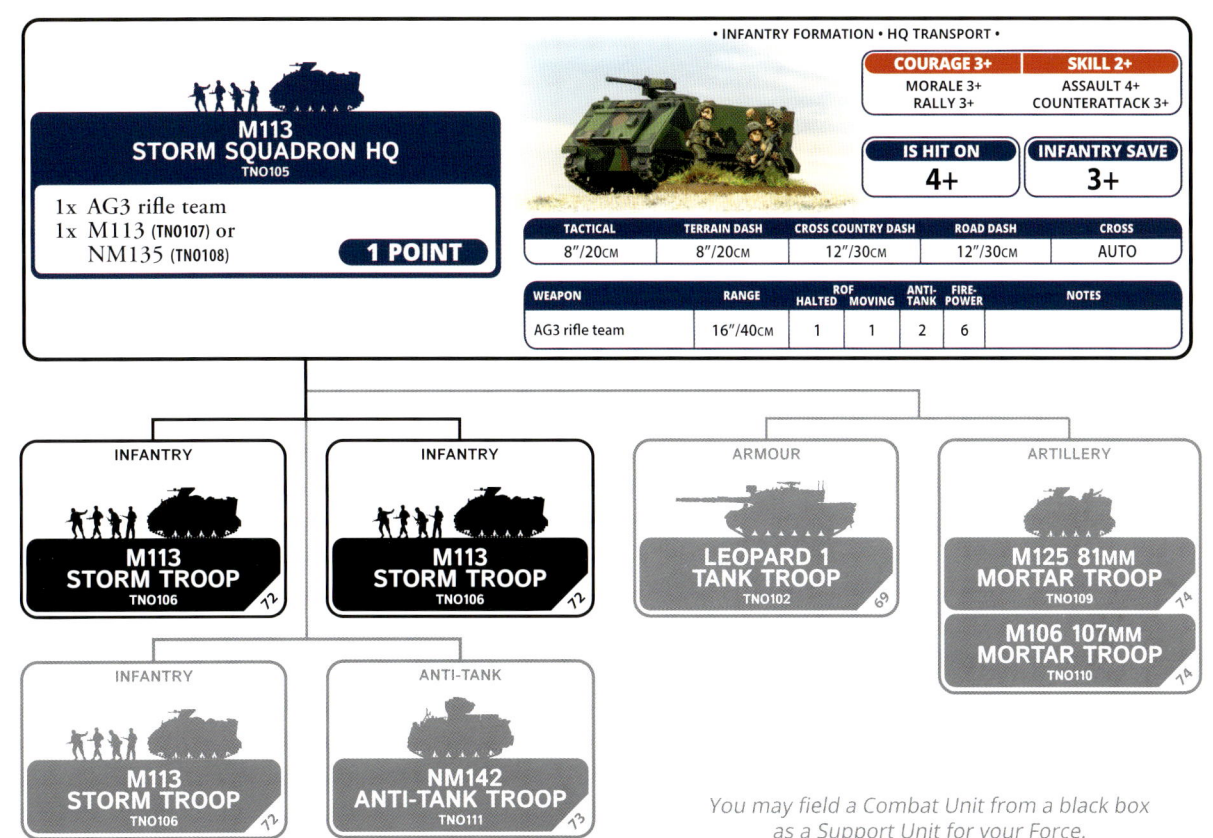

In the mid-1980s the Norwegians reorganised their armoured battalions along Swedish lines as mixed battalions with both tank squadrons and *stormeskadroner* (storm squadrons, mechanised infantry companies). This organisation was introduced into the armoured battalion of Brigade Nord and in two mobilisation battalions, one in eastern Norway and one in Trøndelag (the county surrounding Trondheim). This also marked a change for the mechanised infantry, with the infantry handing over all the M113s to the cavalry arm of which both the tank and storm squadrons were part.

The cavalry's Storm Squadrons now represented the mechanised infantry arm of the Norwegian Army. Unlike other nations where the infantry arm of service formed both light and mechanised infantry, in Norway the mechanised infantry came under the cavalry arm, so by default the armoured arm of service.

The first half of the 1980s also saw the upgrade of the M113s to NM135s, which mounted a small turret with a 20mm cannon and a MG3 7.62mm machine-gun.

BRIGADE NORD
M113 STORM TROOP

M113 STORM TROOP
- 4x MG3 team with M72 LAW anti-tank
- 3x Carl Gustav anti-tank team
- 2x M113 (TN0107)
- 2x NM135 (TN0108)

7 POINTS

- 3x MG3 team with M72 LAW anti-tank
- 2x Carl Gustav anti-tank team
- 1x M113 (TN0107)
- 2x NM135 (TN0108)

5 POINTS

OPTIONS
- Replace all M113 with NM135 (TN0108) transports for +1 point.
- Replace all Carl Gustav anti-tank teams with Eryx anti-tank missile teams for +2 points.

• INFANTRY UNIT •

COURAGE 4+	SKILL 3+
MORALE 4+	ASSAULT 4+
RALLY 4+	COUNTERATTACK 4+

IS HIT ON	INFANTRY SAVE
4+	3+

TACTICAL	TERRAIN DASH	CROSS COUNTRY DASH	ROAD DASH	CROSS
8"/20cm	8"/20cm	12"/30cm	12"/30cm	AUTO

WEAPON	RANGE	ROF HALTED	ROF MOVING	ANTI-TANK	FIRE-POWER	NOTES
MG3 team or	16"/40cm	3	2	2	5+	
M72 LAW anti-tank	12"/30cm	1	1	12	5+	HEAT, Slow Firing
Carl Gustav anti-tank team	16"/40cm	1	1	17	3↑	Assault 5↑, HEAT, Slow Firing
Eryx anti-tank missile team	16"/40cm	1	-	24	4+	Guided, HEAT, No Assault, Tandem Warhead, Thermal Imaging

A Norwegian *Stormtropp* (Storm Troop) is a mechanised infantry unit with the role of working in cooperaton with the tanks of the armoured battalion of which they are an integral part. They are armed with MG3 machineguns, Carl Gustav recoilless anti-tank weapons, G3 battle rifles and 66mm M72 LAW disposible anti-tank rockets. They ride in M113 armoured personel carriers (APC, Norwegian *PPK, pansret personellkjøretøy*) and NM135 infantry fighting vehicles (IFV, Norwegian *SPV, Stormpanservogn*).

The NM135 *stormpanservogn* is rebuilt on the M113 chassis, modified to add a turret on the right side. The turret is armed with a 20mm Rheinmetall autocannon. The NM135 carried an anti-tank group, a machine-gun group, the deputy section leader, and the reserve vehicle commander — who took over when the section commander dismounted from the vehicle commander's position.

When the section disembarked, the vehicle commander switched to the section leader role, and the vehicle could thus operate independently of the infantry section under command of the reserve vehicle commander. The distribution of the unit through the NM135 and M113 transport vehicles can vary from vehicle to vehicle, depending on the wishes of the troop commander.

BRIGADE NORD
M113 TRANSPORT

• TANK ATTACHMENT • AMPHIBIOUS • PASSENGERS 3 •

COURAGE 4+	SKILL 3+
MORALE 4+	ASSAULT 5+
REMOUNT 4+	COUNTERATTACK 5+

IS HIT ON 4+

FRONT	SIDE	TOP
3	2	1

TACTICAL	TERRAIN DASH	CROSS COUNTRY DASH	ROAD DASH	CROSS
10"/25cm	16"/40cm	24"/60cm	32"/80cm	3+

WEAPON	RANGE	ROF HALTED	ROF MOVING	ANTI-TANK	FIRE-POWER
7.62mm AA MG	16"/40cm	3	3	2	6

BRIGADE NORD
NM135 TRANSPORT

• TANK ATTACHMENT • AMPHIBIOUS • INFRA-RED (IR) • PASSENGERS 3 •

COURAGE 4+	SKILL 3+
MORALE 4+	ASSAULT 5+
REMOUNT 4+	COUNTERATTACK 5+

IS HIT ON 4+

FRONT	SIDE	TOP
3	2	1

TACTICAL	TERRAIN DASH	CROSS COUNTRY DASH	ROAD DASH	CROSS
10"/25cm	16"/40cm	24"/60cm	32"/80cm	3+

WEAPON	RANGE	ROF HALTED	ROF MOVING	ANTI-TANK	FIRE-POWER	NOTES
2cm Rh202 gun	20"/50cm	3	2	7	5+	Anti-helicopter
7.62mm AA MG	16"/40cm	3	3	2	6	

Crew: 3 - commander, gunner, driver + 7 passengers
Weight: 28.2 tonnes
Length: 6.79m (22'3")
Width: 3.24m (10'8")
Height: 2.95m (9'9")
Armour: Welded steel 30mm

Weapons: Rheinmetall 20mm Rh 202 Gun
1x MG3 7.62mm MG
Speed: 75 km/h (47 mph)
Engine: MB 833 Ea-500 V6 turbo diesel engine, 600 hp (447 kW)
Range: 520 km (323 miles)

BRIGADE NORD
NM142 ANTI-TANK TROOP

NM142 ANTI-TANK TROOP	
4x NM142 (iTOW)	8 POINTS
2x NM142 (iTOW)	4 POINTS
4x NM142 (TOW-2)	9 POINTS
2x NM142 (TOW-2)	5 POINTS

• TANK UNIT • AMPHIBIOUS • HAMMERHEAD • THERMAL IMAGING •

COURAGE 4+	SKILL 3+
MORALE 4+	ASSAULT 5+
REMOUNT 4+	COUNTERATTACK 5+

IS HIT ON 4+

FRONT	SIDE	TOP
3	2	1

TACTICAL	TERRAIN DASH	CROSS COUNTRY DASH	ROAD DASH	CROSS
10"/25CM	16"/40CM	24"/60CM	32"/80CM	3+

WEAPON	RANGE	ROF HALTED	ROF MOVING	ANTI-TANK	FIRE-POWER	NOTES
Improved TOW missile	8"/20CM - 48"/120CM	1	-	21	3+	Guided, HEAT
TOW-2 missile	8"/20CM - 48"/120CM	1	-	23	3+	Guided, HEAT
7.62mm AA MG	16"/40CM	3	3	2	6	

NM142 is a Norwegian missile tank-hunter vehicle (*Rakettpanserjager*) based on the M113 APC. The NM142 mounts a turret containing a TOW guided anti-tank missile system, with one launch tube on each side of the turret in a concept broadly similar to the US M901. This TOW turret was developed in Norway by the Kværner Eureka engineering company.

The commander's hatch mounts an MG3 machine-gun as a secondary armament. The NM142 has a crew of four, a commander, a gunner, loader, and driver.

Usually, a *Panserverntropp* (anti-tank troop) consists of four NM142s, led by a lieutenant. Individual troops are incorporated in various mechanised formations.

BRIGADE NORD
M125 81mm MORTAR TROOP

M125 81MM MORTAR TROOP	
4x M125	**3 POINTS**

M125 Bombekastervogn (mortar vehicle) is the Norwegian variant of the M125 mortar carrier similar to the *M106 bombekastervogn*, but armed with a 81mm *NM95 bombekaster* (mortar).

The M125 81mm mortar carriers provide the Storm Troops with mobile on-call artillery. The squadron can direct fire and smoke bombardments quickly when required by the battlefield situation.

• TANK UNIT • AMPHIBIOUS •

COURAGE 4+	SKILL 3+
MORALE 4+	ASSAULT 6
REMOUNT 4+	COUNTERATTACK 6

IS HIT ON 4+
FRONT	SIDE	TOP
3	2	0

TACTICAL	TERRAIN DASH	CROSS COUNTRY DASH	ROAD DASH	CROSS
10"/25cm	16"/40cm	24"/60cm	32"/80cm	3+

WEAPON	RANGE	ROF HALTED	ROF MOVING	ANTI-TANK	FIRE-POWER	NOTES
81mm mortar	56"/140cm	ARTILLERY		1	4+	Smoke Bombardment
7.62mm AA MG	16"/40cm	3	3	2	6	

BRIGADE NORD
M106 107mm MORTAR TROOP

M106 107MM MORTAR TROOP	
4x M106 107mm	**4 POINTS**
2x M106 107mm	**2 POINTS**

The Norwegians also fielded the M106 mortar carrier, or *M106 bombekastervogn* (mortar vehicle) as they designated it. It mounted the orginal American M30 107mm heavy mortar.

• TANK UNIT • AMPHIBIOUS •

COURAGE 4+	SKILL 3+
MORALE 4+	ASSAULT 6
REMOUNT 4+	COUNTERATTACK 6

IS HIT ON 4+
FRONT	SIDE	TOP
3	2	0

TACTICAL	TERRAIN DASH	CROSS COUNTRY DASH	ROAD DASH	CROSS
10"/25cm	16"/40cm	24"/60cm	32"/80cm	3+

WEAPON	RANGE	ROF HALTED	ROF MOVING	ANTI-TANK	FIRE-POWER	NOTES
M30 107mm mortar	48"/120cm	ARTILLERY		2	4+	Smoke Bombardment
.50 cal AA MG	20"/50cm	3	2	4	5+	

NORWEGIAN SUPPORT UNITS

FELTVOGN (TOW) ANTI-TANK SECTION
BRIGADE NORD

FELTVOGN (TOW) ANTI-TANK SECTION	
2x 240GD Feltvogn (iTOW)	**2 POINTS**

• UNARMOURED TANK UNIT • SCOUT • THERMAL IMAGING •

COURAGE 4+	SKILL 3+
MORALE 4+ RALLY 4+	ASSAULT - COUNTERATTACK -

IS HIT ON	TANK SAVE
4+	4+

TACTICAL	TERRAIN DASH	CROSS COUNTRY DASH	ROAD DASH	CROSS
10"/25cm	12"/30cm	20"/50cm	48"/120cm	4+

WEAPON	RANGE	ROF HALTED	ROF MOVING	ANTI-TANK	FIRE-POWER	NOTES
Improved TOW missile	8"/20cm – 48"/120cm	1	-	21	3+	HEAT, Guided
7.62mm AA MG	16"/40cm	3	3	2	6	

The Norwegian Army used a variety of light utility vehicles, or field cars (*Feltvogn*), the newest of which is the West German Mercedes-Benz 240GD Geländewagen.

As well as reconnaissance, some of these vehicles are used to carry and mount the Improved TOW anti-tank missile system, where it could be mounted in the rear.

NM195 AIR DEFENCE BATTERY
BRIGADE NORD

NM195 AIR DEFENCE BATTERY	
4x NM195 (RBS-70)	**6 POINTS**
2x NM195 (RBS-70)	**3 POINTS**

• TANK UNIT • AMPHIBIOUS • THERMAL IMAGING •

COURAGE 4+	SKILL 3+
MORALE 4+ REMOUNT 4+	ASSAULT 5+ COUNTERATTACK 5+

IS HIT ON 4+		
FRONT	SIDE	TOP
3	2	0

TACTICAL	TERRAIN DASH	CROSS COUNTRY DASH	ROAD DASH	CROSS
10"/25cm	16"/40cm	24"/60cm	32"/80cm	3+

WEAPON	RANGE	ROF HALTED	ROF MOVING	ANTI-TANK	FIRE-POWER	NOTES
RBS-70 missile	56"/140cm	2	-	-	4+	Guided AA
7.62mm AA MG	16"/40cm	3	3	2	6	

A *Luftvernbatteri* (air defence battery) of the Light Air Defence Artillery (LLA) of Brigade Nord is equipped with the Swedish Robot 70 system (RBS-70), which works with the the separate Giraffe search radar system situated behind the front lines. The RBS-70 missile launchers are mounted on the NM195 air defence vehicle (a modified M113 APC).

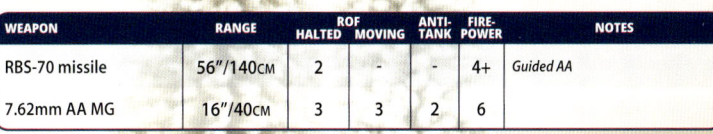

BRIGADE NORD
M109 FIELD ARTILLERY BATTERY

M109 FIELD ARTILLERY BATTERY	
6x M109G	14 POINTS
3x M109G	7 POINTS
6x M109A3GN	16 POINTS
3x M109A3GN	8 POINTS

Norway procured 126 M109G from West Germany. During the 1980s a program was begun to upgrade these to M109A3GN and the vehicles received, among other things, new and longer M185 155mm howitzers.

• TANK UNIT •

COURAGE 4+	SKILL 3+
MORALE 4+	ASSAULT 5+
REMOUNT 4+	COUNTERATTACK 5+

IS HIT ON 4+
FRONT 2 | SIDE 2 | TOP 1

TACTICAL	TERRAIN DASH	CROSS COUNTRY DASH	ROAD DASH	CROSS
10"/25CM	16"/40CM	24"/60CM	28"/70CM	3+

WEAPON	RANGE	ROF HALTED	ROF MOVING	ANTI-TANK	FIRE-POWER	NOTES
M109G 155mm howitzer	88"/220CM	ARTILLERY		4	2+	Smoke Bombardment
or Direct fire	24"/60CM	1	1	12	1+	Brutal, Slow Firing, Smoke
M109A3GN 155mm howitzer	96"/240CM	ARTILLERY		4	2+	Smoke Bombardment
or Direct fire	36"/90CM	1	1	15	1+	Brutal, Slow Firing, Smoke
.50 cal AA MG	20"/50CM	3	2	4	5+	

Crew: 6 - commander, 2x gunner, 2x loader, driver
Weight: 25.5 tonnes
Length: 9.1m (30')
Width: 3.15m (10'4")
Height: 3.25m (10'8")
Armour: 20mm

Weapons: M109 M126 155mm howitzer or M109A3GN M185 155mm howitzer
.50 cal AA MG
Speed: 56 km/h (35 mph)
Engine: Detroit Diesel 8V71T diesel, 450 hp (335.56 kW)
Range: 350 km (216 miles)

BRIGADE NORD
M113 OP FORWARD OBSERVER

M113 OP FORWARD OBSERVER	
1x M113 OP	1 POINT

You must field:
• a M106 107mm Mortar Troop (TN0110), or
• a M109 Field Artillery Battery (TN0116)
before you may field a M113 OP.

The NM201 *Ildlederpanservogn, artilleri* (Fire Control Armoured Vehicle, Artillery) is a Norwegian variant of the M113 used by artillery forward observers.

• INDEPENDENT TANK UNIT • AMPHIBIOUS • INFRA-RED (IR) • OBSERVER • SCOUT •

COURAGE 4+	SKILL 3+
MORALE 4+	ASSAULT 5+
REMOUNT 4+	COUNTERATTACK 5+

IS HIT ON 4+
FRONT 3 | SIDE 2 | TOP 1

TACTICAL	TERRAIN DASH	CROSS COUNTRY DASH	ROAD DASH	CROSS
10"/25CM	16"/40CM	24"/60CM	32"/80CM	3+

WEAPON	RANGE	ROF HALTED	ROF MOVING	ANTI-TANK	FIRE-POWER	NOTES
7.62mm AA MG	16"/40CM	3	3	2	6	

BRIGADE NORD
FELTVOGN RECON TROOP

FELTVOGN RECON TROOP	
3x 240GD Feltvogn (7.62mm AA MG) 2x 240GD Feltvogn (.50 cal AA MG)	**3 POINTS**
2x 240GD Feltvogn (7.62mm AA MG) 1x 240GD Feltvogn (.50 cal AA MG)	**2 POINTS**

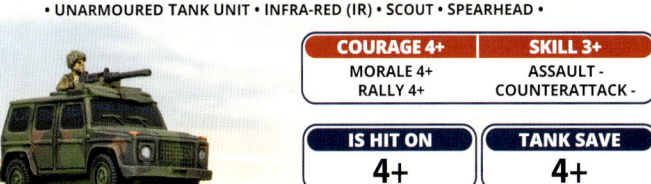

• UNARMOURED TANK UNIT • INFRA-RED (IR) • SCOUT • SPEARHEAD •

COURAGE 4+	SKILL 3+
MORALE 4+ RALLY 4+	ASSAULT - COUNTERATTACK -

IS HIT ON	TANK SAVE
4+	4+

TACTICAL	TERRAIN DASH	CROSS COUNTRY DASH	ROAD DASH	CROSS
10"/25cm	12"/30cm	20"/50cm	48"/120cm	4+

WEAPON	RANGE	ROF HALTED	ROF MOVING	ANTI-TANK	FIRE-POWER	NOTES
7.62mm AA MG	16"/40cm	3	3	2	6	
.50 cal AA MG	20"/50cm	3	2	4	5+	

Norwegian *Feltvogn* is a term used for light cross-county vehicles like the West German Mercedes-Benz 240GD Geländewagen. As well as general utility, *Feltvogn* vehicles were used for reconnaissance and patrolling.

BRIGADE NORD
NM135 RECON TROOP

NM135 RECON TROOP	
3x NM135 Scout	**3 POINTS**

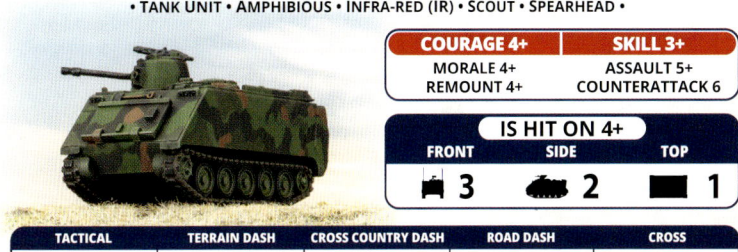

• TANK UNIT • AMPHIBIOUS • INFRA-RED (IR) • SCOUT • SPEARHEAD •

COURAGE 4+	SKILL 3+
MORALE 4+ REMOUNT 4+	ASSAULT 5+ COUNTERATTACK 6

IS HIT ON 4+		
FRONT	SIDE	TOP
3	2	1

TACTICAL	TERRAIN DASH	CROSS COUNTRY DASH	ROAD DASH	CROSS
10"/25cm	16"/40cm	24"/60cm	32"/80cm	3+

WEAPON	RANGE	ROF HALTED	ROF MOVING	ANTI-TANK	FIRE-POWER	NOTES
2cm Rh202 gun	20"/50cm	3	2	7	5+	Anti-helicopter
7.62mm AA MG	16"/40cm	3	3	2	6	

As well as being used as an Infantry Fighting Vehicle, the NM135 also saw service as a reconnaissance vehicle in small numbers with a troop of three vehicles allocated to each of the brigades.

US MARINE CORPS
AV-8 HARRIER ATTACK FLIGHT

AV-8 HARRIER ATTACK FLIGHT	
4x AV-8 Harrier	**6 POINTS**
2x AV-8 Harrier	**3 POINTS**

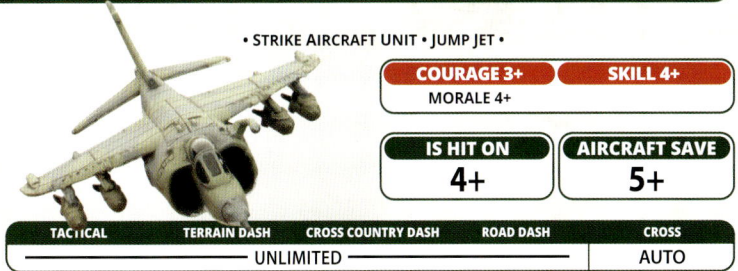

• STRIKE AIRCRAFT UNIT • JUMP JET •

COURAGE 3+	SKILL 4+
MORALE 4+	

IS HIT ON	AIRCRAFT SAVE
4+	5+

TACTICAL	TERRAIN DASH	CROSS COUNTRY DASH	ROAD DASH	CROSS
— UNLIMITED —				AUTO

WEAPON	RANGE	ROF HALTED	ROF MOVING	ANTI-TANK	FIRE-POWER	NOTES
30mm Aden gun	8"/20cm	-	3	7	5+	Anti-helicopter
CBU-100 cluster bomb	6"/15cm	SALVO		7	5+	

The US Marine Corps adopted the British Hawker-Siddley Harrier, the famed 'Jump Jet'. Designated AV-8, the Harrier is a high performance jet aircraft that is uniquely capable of vertical and short take off and landing (VSTOL). It does this by swivelling its exhaust nozzles down to allow it land vertically or to reduce the required distance for take off.

The Marines can operate their Harriers from aircraft carriers as well as light assault ships. Once inland the Harriers operate from forward bases, containing one to four aircraft, located 20 miles (32 km) from the front, while a more established airbase would be located around 50 miles (80 km) from the front. These forward bases allow for a far greater sortie rate and reduced fuel consumption.

Armed with an electrically-powered 30mm Aden 5-chamber revolver cannon and CBU-100 cluster bombs, the Harrier can deal with both air and ground targets.

JUMP JET
US Marine AV-8 Harrier jump jets can get airborne with a full armament load after a short take-off run. This allows it to operate from hidden locations near the front, ideal for Norwegian conditions.

> Jump Jet Strike Aircraft arrive each turn on a roll of 3+, rather than the usual 4+.

NORWEGIAN BASING & PAINTING

BASING NORWEGIAN INFANTRY

Formation Command AG3 rifle team

Base the Commander on a small base with a radio operator and rifleman.

Carl Gustav anti-tank team

Eryx anti-tank missile teams

Base Carl Gustav anti-tank and Eryx anti-tank missile teams on a small base with a gunner and an assistant.

MG3 team with M72 LAW anti-tank

Base Norwegian Infantry teams on a medium base. Teams combine a machine-gunner armed with a light machine-gun, and riflemen armed with rifles and light anti-tank weapons. Unit Leaders replace the machine-gun and a rifleman with an officer and radio operator.

NORWEGIAN TANKS

- Olive Green (967)
- Flat Earth (983)
- Cam. Olive Green (894)
- Black Grey (862)

Norwegian Infantry

- *Flesh* — **Flat Flesh (955)**
- **Beige Brown (875)**
- *Camo Smock Base* — **Yellow Green (954)**
- *Camo Smock Camouflage* — **Ger. Cam. Med. Brown (826)**
- *Camo Smock Camouflage* — **Luftwaffe Cam. Green (823)**
- *Webbing & Painted Metal* — **Olive Drab (887)**
- *Uniform* — **Russian Uniform (924)**
- *Boots & Rifles* — **Black Grey (862)**

US Marine Aircraft

- **Medium Sea Grey (870)**
- **Olive Drab (887)**
- **Field Blue (964)**
- **White (870)**

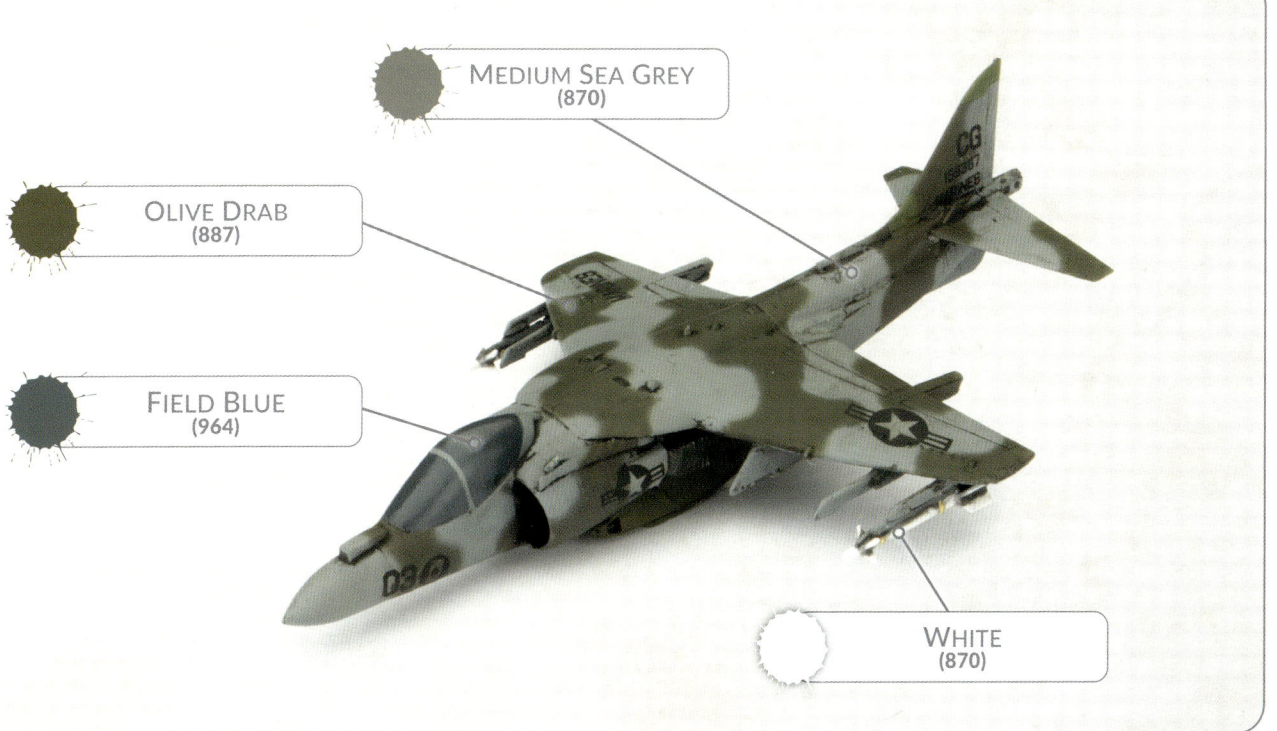

NORWEGIAN BASING & PAINTING

79

NORWEGIAN & DANISH CATALOGUE

The following pages contain a catalogue of all the miniatures that are available to Norwegian and Danish forces.

Norwegian and Danish forces use products from the following nations' catalogues:

 NORWEGIAN    SWEDISH   NATO

 WEST GERMAN   AMERICAN

TNA950

Nordic Forces Decals

 **Norwegian Unit Cards** — WW3-08N
CONTAINS: 16x Norwegian Unit Cards, and 11x Allied Support Unit Cards.

Danish Unit Cards — WW3-08D
CONTAINS: 16x Danish Unit Cards, and 12x Allied Support Unit Cards.

TGBX14

Danish Leopard 1

Norwegian Leopard 1

ALL PLASTIC

CONTAINS:
5x Leopard 1 Tanks

WEST GERMAN — **Leopard 1 Panzer Zug**

TSWBX02

Centurion (20 pdr)
Centurion DK (105mm)

ALL PLASTIC

CONTAINS:
5x Centurion or Centurion DK Tanks

SWEDISH — Centurion Tank Platoon

TUBX24

ALL PLASTIC

CONTAINS:
3x M109 155mm Self-propelled Howitzers

AMERICAN — M109 Field Artillery Battery

TNOBX03

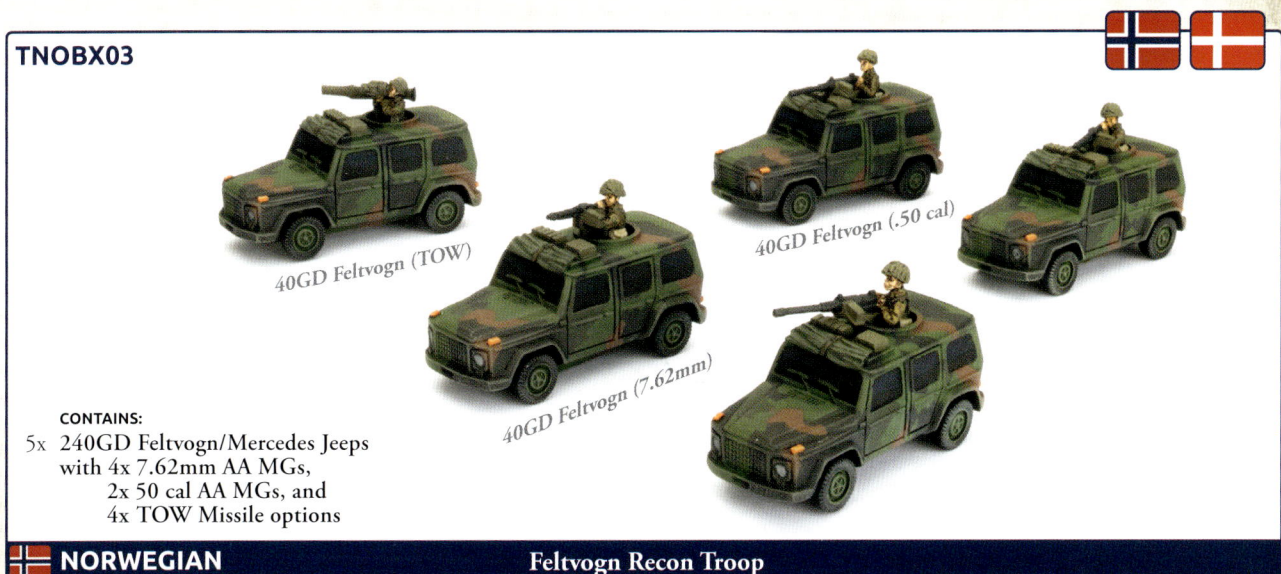

40GD Feltvogn (TOW)
40GD Feltvogn (.50 cal)
40GD Feltvogn (7.62mm)

CONTAINS:
5x 240GD Feltvogn/Mercedes Jeeps with 4x 7.62mm AA MGs, 2x 50 cal AA MGs, and 4x TOW Missile options

NORWEGIAN — Feltvogn Recon Troop

TNOBX02

CONTAINS:
4x NM142 Tank-hunters

🇳🇴 NORWEGIAN — NM142 Anti-tank Troop

TNO702

CONTAINS:
- 1x G3 rifle team
- 4x MG3 team with M72 LAW anti-tank
- 3x Carl Gustav anti-tank teams
- 3x Eryx anti-tank missile teams

Note: Danish Carl Gustav teams are based diferently to Norwegian Carl Gustav anti-tank teams, See Danish basing guide on page 106.

🇳🇴 NORWEGIAN — M113 Storm Troop

TNOBX01

CONTAINS:
4x NM135 Transports or
NM195 RBS-70 AA Missile Carriers

🇳🇴 NORWEGIAN — NM135 or NM195 Platoon

TGBX09

CONTAINS:
3x M113 Transports,
   M125 81mm Mortar, or
   M106 107 mm Mortar

WEST GERMAN — M113 Panzermörser Zug

TGR708

CONTAINS:
6x Redeye AA Missile Teams

WEST GERMAN — Fliegerfaust Gruppe

TNBX03

CONTAINS:
5x M113 TOW

NATO — NATO M113 Transports

TGBX15

CONTAINS:
2x Tornado Aircraft
2x Flight Stands
4x Rare-earth Magnets
1x Decal Sheet

WEST GERMAN — Tornado Strike Flight

TUBX12

CONTAINS:
2x Harrier Aircraft
2x Flight Stands
4x Rare-earth Magnets
1x Decal Sheet

AMERICAN — AV-8 Harrier Attack Flight

FORCES IN WORLD WAR III

9 APRIL 1940 AND THE OCCUPATION

Denmark avoided becoming embroiled in the First World War by declaring neutrality. It repeated this step at the outbreak of the Second World War, however this measure proved insufficient, and on 9 April 1940 the country was occupied by Germany. The closing days of the war in May 1945 were marked with great nervousness, as it was uncertain whether Denmark would be liberated from the west or east, and what consequences liberation would bring. The military resistance groups and the Danish Brigade occupied the key central political locations. In the event, liberation came from the west and the democratic system was re-established. At the same time, an extremely difficult reconstruction of the Danish Army was initiated.

MEMBERSHIP OF NATO

In the immediate post-war years, the Nordic countries negotiated to form a defence federation, but nothing came to fruition. Instead, Denmark and Norway chose in 1949, under the ever-worsening cold war between East and West, to join the Western Alliance in the form of NATO. Membership demanded a significant military structure, which was implemented through the ambitious *forsvarsordning* (defence system). Denmark was aided in this army restucturing with weapons aid from the United States and Canada.

The army was divided into a Field Army that would be the first mobile land defence, and a regional defence that would constitute a localised defence force. The Field Army consisted of a corps in each of the regions, *Østre Korps* (Eastern Corps) and *Vestre Korps* (Western Corps), each with several divisions and corps troops units.

The divisions contained a number of regimental battlegroups/brigades and divisional troops. In addition, *Bornholms Værn* (Bornholm Defence) was formed, which was brigade sized and included units of all arms. At the beginning of the 1950s, the initial training period was set to 18 months to prepare combat ready army units. Regional defence consisted of eight regions, whose units were partly formed by the Army as local defence battalions (infantry battalions) and filled out by the newly created Home Guard, of which there was a very large number of companies.

In the 1950s, the defence of Denmark was integrated into NATO's command system. This was based on the common NATO command for the whole of Europe that would take effect during wartime, with a system of local commands below that. However, a Danish transition to NATO command required the *Folketing* (parliament) to approve it, but regional defence would remain under national command. The total war that was the reality during the two world wars became the starting point for the building of a Danish total defence in the 1950s.

MOTORISATION AND MODERNISATION

During the 1950s and 1960s the framework was laid for a radical motorisation of the Army, where both combat and combat support units were increasingly motorised, allowing for a much more mobile type of warfare. A prerequisite for this was the expansion of the Army's control and communication systems with new radios and other signalling equipment.

With *forsvarsordningen* 1960, a further reorganisation of the army began. The field army now primarily consisted of six armoured infantry brigades, where tanks and armoured infantry formed the core.

During 1950s West Germany had become a member of NATO, and German military units quickly became an important part of the defence of the Danish-North German region. In 1962, a Danish-German unitary command for the NATO forces in Denmark and Schleswig-Holstein was established to lead forces in wartime.

With regard to the land defence, Denmark was divided into two: a command for the land defensive of Schleswig-Holstein and Denmark west of the Great Belt, and a command for Denmark eastward. During wartime, the two commands would take over the leadership role that the two Danish corps had previously had.

THE ARMY IN THE 1970s AND 1980s

The Warsaw Pact's military structure in the 1960s necessitated ever-increasing Western preparedness. In Denmark, this was implemented through *forsvarsordningen* 1973, where an increased number of professional, permanent soldiers formed the core of brigades and other units. The professional soldiers strengthened the standing force and could handle the increasingly complicated weapon systems and equipment. Conversely, the number of conscripts and their education time was reduced. The conscripts were removed from the standing force, but still made up the majority of mobilisation forces. The 1973 reforms largely remained in place for the rest of the Cold War, but in the 1980s, the number of conscripts and their education time increased again.

During the 1970s, the army's doctrine became focused on a *"stedbunden forsvarskamp"* (place-based defence battle) with more use of field fortifications such as minefields and other obstacles, and the demolition of bridges. In addition, allied reinforcements became more important for the defence of the Jutland and northern West German territory, where the Danish-German corps, LANDJUT, with Jyske Division and the West German 6th Panzergrenadier Division, were to conduct the important defensive battles in Schleswig-Holstein and Southern Jutland.

JYSKE DIVISION

Since D-Day +1, Danish forces have been struggling with the landings from the combined Soviet and Polish Marines. Fortunately, support from the Bundeswehr was expected to be in transit, having been promised long before the outbreak of hostilities. Armoured forces had been sent to rapidly reinforce the line.

As part of the rush to the coastline, Danish Dragonregiment's Leopards have been crucial in slowing the Warsaw Pact forces' inland rush. Combined arms practice down to company and squadron level has paid off with the Danes giving better than they have been hit with.

The scrubby marshes of the Danish coastline have been perfectly suited to the lighter Leopard 1A3 in Danish service, proving more than capable of crushing the older T-55 variants the enemy have thrown into action. Profligate use of iTOW missiles have been invaluable with the missile systems having no problem with terminating even the best of the landing force's armoured threats.

However, the smaller Danish mechanised infantry platoons have been feeling undergunned when facing four and five times their number, especially the Soviet "Black Death" Marine Landing Forces. The enemy's reputation for stubborn persistence had proven well deserved.

Isolated groups of Danish infantry have embedded themselves in the picture-perfect townships near the coastline. Like ticks in the hide of an elephant, they harass and torment the invaders constantly. It was on the outskirts of the garrison town of Fredericia that a battalion of the Kongens Jyske Fodregiment had made their stand. This unit was composed of two mechanised companies in M113s and one squadron of Leopard 1A3s. Support from a tank destroyer unit in ancient Centurions with outdated 20pdr guns had tipped the scales in favour of the defenders. Massive casualties from careful aimed fire had proven disastrous for the Soviet Marines landing in this area. With a ferocity few expected of the conscripts, the Danes were determined to hold on until their West German allies in 6. Panzergrenadierdivision arrived.

Jyske Division (Jutland Division) was originally formed in 1952, then called the 3rd Division. Initially it had one standing brigade and two reserve brigades. In 1962 it was renamed to Jyske Division and by 1975 the two reserve brigades entered into the standing force. The Jyske Division was responsible for the defence of the Jutland Peninsula and constituted the second half of the two main components in the LANDJUT (NATO Allied Land Forces Schleswig-Holstein and Jutland) Corps. In case of rising tensions between the west and the east, the division would start the mobilisation of its reserve forces and deploy its three brigades into their forward defensive positions, in and around Schleswig-Holstein, where they would meet up with their West German counterparts.

Each of the three brigades was made up of one tank battalion, two mechanised infantry battalions, and one artillery battalion. Furthermore, each brigade had an armoured engineering company assigned to it. A Danish tank battalion was made up of two tank squadrons and one mechanised infantry company, while each mechanised infantry battalion comprised two mechanised infantry companies and one tank squadron.

The division also had one motorised infantry battalion, one armoured reconnaissance battalion, one tank destroyer battalion, and one air defence battalion, all of which could be deployed across the area of operations as needed. Due to its role in LANDJUT and the expectations of an armoured push across Schleswig-Holstein and up the Jutland Peninsula to cut off Denmark from the rest of NATO, the Jyske Division's tank and mechanised infantry battalions were the only battalions equipped with the Leopard 1A3, the most modern main battle tank in the Danish arsenal.

ANSGAR'S PANSERINFANTERI

OPENING ROUNDS

Kaptajn Mads Ansgar shook his head to wake himself up. "How long have I been laying here?" was the question going through his head. No matter what the actual answer was, the last few days were a blur for the Danish company commander. As soon as the call for mobilisation had gone out Kaptajn Ansgar had his orders to move his mechanised infantry company into West Germany and wait for the invasion. While in transit the men listened to the news in their M113 tracks, hearing about the first blows of the war much further to the south.

Arriving at the head of the Jutland Division (*Jyske Division* in Danish), Ansgar was told to place his unit just South East of Arhensbok, protecting the vital *Bundesstraße 432* which ran parallel to the West German frontier. Finding a wooded area just south of Bobs, Ansgar had his men debus and he ordered his attached M113 TOW tracks into positions facing east. "Dig in" was the order he gave, knowing that he did not need to highlight the order with a sense of urgency. His men, all professional soldiers, knew what was likely to happen next.

Not long after his men had built foxholes and cover for their tracks in the woods, the radios that connected him to his company's M113s and up to his battalion headquarters started to come alive, not with orders and SITREPs, but with the hum of static. This meant one thing: things are about to get interesting. Why else would the Reds be jamming them? Sending runners to give his orders, Ansgar instructed his troops not to fire until his TOW gunners fired their first shots. After this Ansgar picked a spot on the edge of the woods and scanned the horizon; a spot where he lost track of time.

Around dawn the first signs telling Ansgar something was up was the sputter of a smoking West German Bo-105 PAH. From Ansgar's position it was hard to tell if the pilot was tilting his rotors to warn Ansgar of the enemy or just the desperate attempts of the pilot to control his aircraft. As the helicopter disappeared into the distance, Ansgar heard the voice of Oversergent Knudsen; "what do you think that was all about?"

"I don't know, Anders. Any word from headquarters?" Ansgar replied.

"No sir, nothing at all," was Knudsen's response.

With the exchange over, Ansgar returned to scan the ground in front of him.

Doing his best to keep awake, Ansgar felt like he drifted off for a minute, however in the distance he could hear a low and steady rumble. That could be friend or foe? With the radio jamming he had little idea where other units were or if the Soviets were west of the Elbe–Lübeck Canal. Ansgar scanned the terrain harder and as he moved his binoculars all the way to the right he saw a sight that made any further thoughts of sleep disappear.

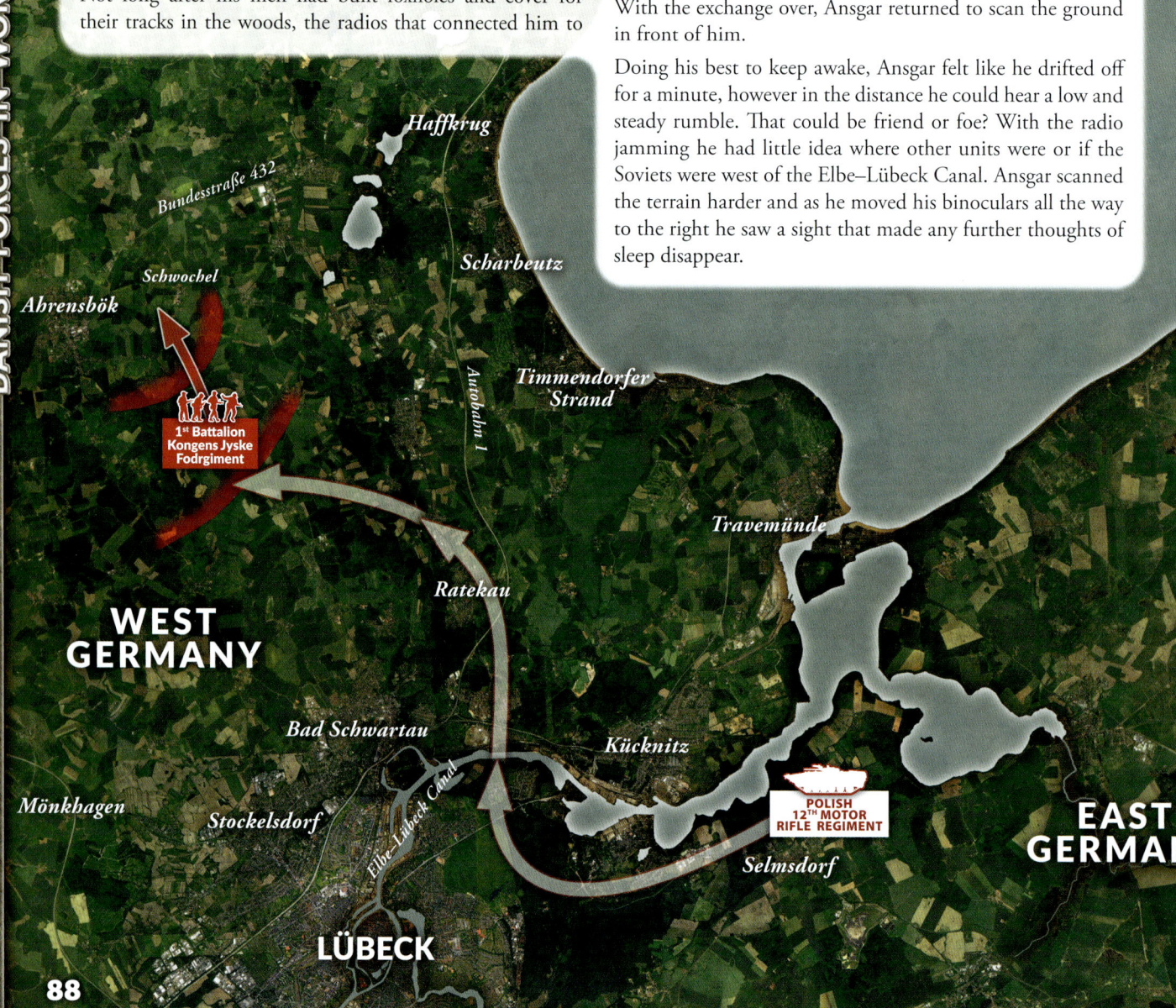

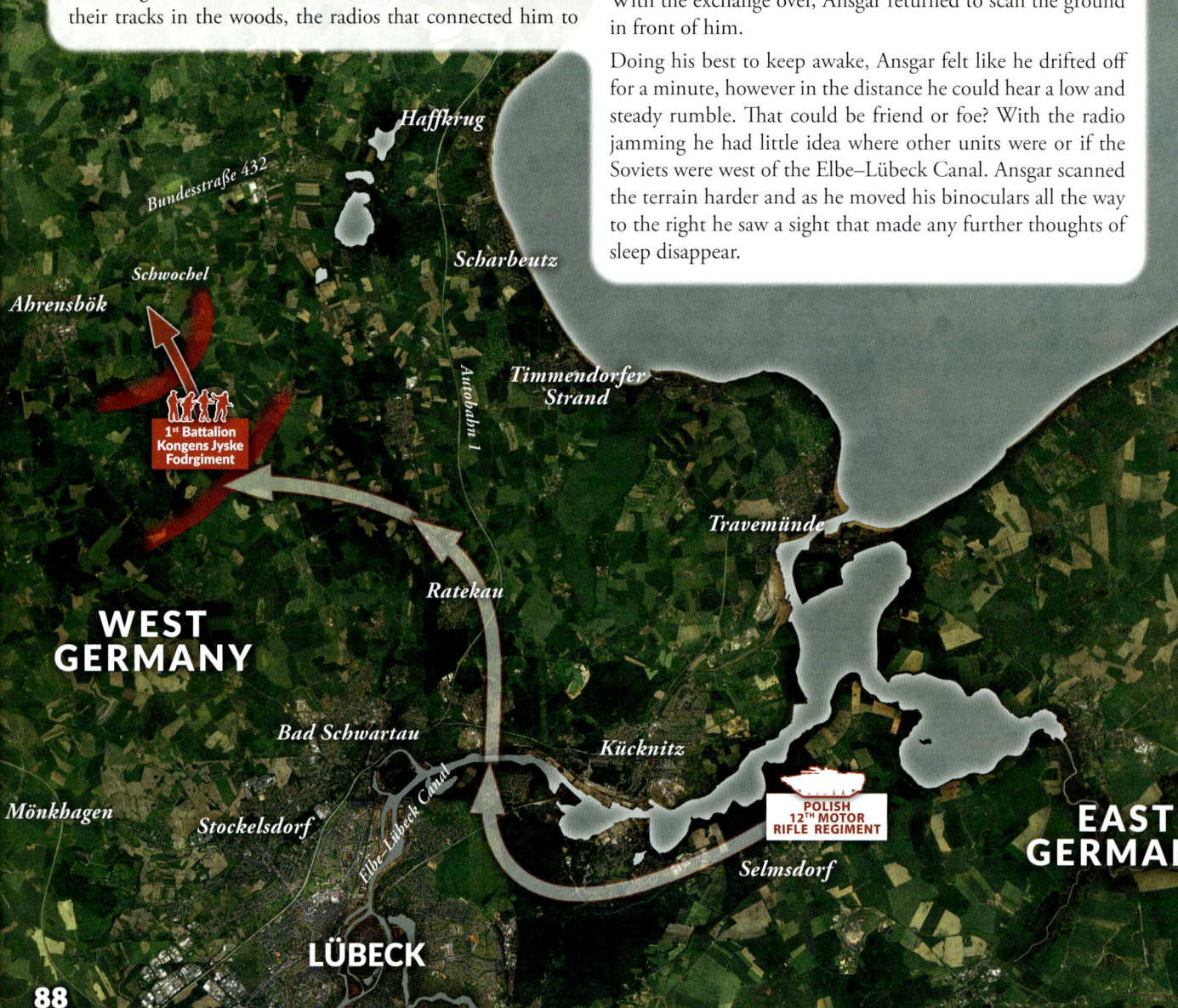

Off in the distance, his trained eyes made out tanks. Low silhouetted, with round turrets, these were unquestionably Warsaw Pact tanks. The tanks were heading south west, right for his company. Each time Ansgar tried to count the tanks, more appeared. It seemed like a whole tank battalion was falling into his lap. As they got closer, Ansgar knew his instincts had been correct. These were T-55s, a ton of them.

"Korporal Andersen! Radio battalion, at least 30 T-55s are heading right for our positions!" Ansgar yelled.

"I am trying sir, we are still jammed!"

As the slow formation seemingly made a bee-line for his position, he saw the lead tanks stop, causing all of the T-55s following them to stop suddenly. After a few seconds the tanks in the front shifted their facing, and the whole formation now took a westerly course right in front of his company's position in the woods. "They seem to be lost" Ansgar thought, which makes sense since he did not see the BMPs or BRDMs of the enemy's reconnnaisance units leading the way.

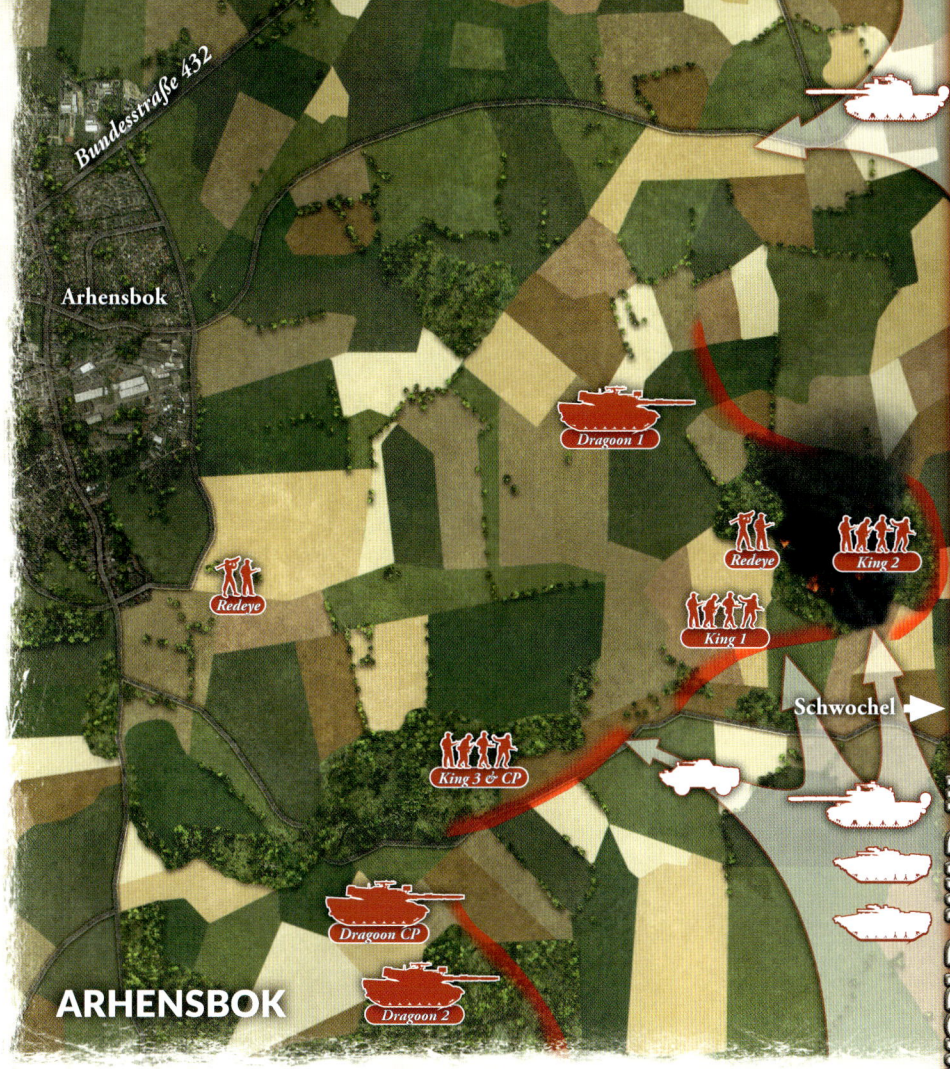

As the formation turned its side to him, Ansgar could make out the red and white symbol of the Polish Army. Poles? How did they get so far west with hostilities being less than three days old? While weighing that question, Ansgar heard a "woosh" and saw a TOW missile from a position to his left head for the enemy mob. Other missiles soon joined it, reaching out for the mass of tanks.

Ansgar looked through his binoculars again and saw that his missile men were scoring hits. Three T-55s were burning viscously, a few others throwing a huge amount of black smoke in the air, and as he turned his head he saw the turret flying through the air.

The mass of T-55 seemed to stop all at once, and as if they were all somehow connected, the survivors turned back to a course that headed straight for Ansgar's position.

ANSGAR PULLS BACK

Kaptajn Ansgar knew that his unit's luck could not last much longer with the T-55s bearing down on them. He was about to call his runner over to tell his company to fall back when his world turned upside down. He was showered with soil and foliage, leaving his ears ringing. He looked towards the Polish unit, noticing they had stopped. The Poles were firing on his unit's location, and one of the enemy's shells had landed close to his position. Despite the loss of hearing and disorientation, Ansgar made his way to Korporal Andersen's position behind his own. The woods were now alive with explosions that threw broken trees, branches, and earth in the air.

Ansgar moved to where he thought his command M113 was, only to find it gone. Just as he was contemplating his next move he felt someone tug on his shoulder. It was Knudsen, who was obviously yelling, but Ansgar couldn't hear anything aside from the ringing. Ansgar's Oversergent quickly realised that his commander was in bad shape and pulled him by the arm deeper into the woods to a trail where the command track was sitting, all ready to move out.

As Knudsen pulled his wounded commander into the M113, Ansgar yelled "What is our status?"

Knudsen, knowing Ansgar could not hear, held up a finger to say "Give me a moment". Ansgar felt the track lurch forward and pick up speed. Ansgar reached for his map to remind his Oversergent the predesignated fallback position just north of Arhensbok. Knudsen nodded his head that he understood and donned the headset for the radio and spoke into the microphone. After a moment Knudsen gave him a thumbs up, which Ansgar took as a sign that the radio net was operational once again.

As Knudsen started to jot notes on a pad, Ansgar felt the track rumble as if he was in an earthquake. Knudsen then handed him the pad he had been writing on. Ansgar read it; Troops 1, 2 and 3 pulling out, Troop 3 down to one M113 and eight personnel, no contact from the Mortar Troop.

Troop 3 had been on the northern most edge of the woods and had borne the brunt of the enemy's fire. Starting to regain his senses, Ansgar popped his head out of the hatch on top of the M113, looking back to the woods where his unit had been just a few moments before. He knew that they had just barely escaped total destruction.

THE DANES REGROUP

As Ansgar's M113 raced to the rally point, his senses including his hearing returned. The 11 kilometre trip took longer than expected. Despite the fact that the war had been going on for over a day already, many civilians had been slow to leave and the roads were clogged with terrified Germans heading west. A West German *Polizei* checkpoint at Schwochel stopped the convoy long enough for Ansgar to orient himself on a map and gave the lead vehicle a good route to the rally point.

He noted a familiar sight as he closed in on the rally point: the Leopard tanks of the Jutland Dragoon Regiment (*Jydske Dragonregiment*). When he got closer, he saw the friendly face of *Premierløjtnant* Hans Johansen, a tank company commander in the Jutland Dragoons. His M113 slowed down as it approached the tanks and Johansen shouted to Ansgar, "Mads, what the heck happened up there?"

Ansgar just shook his head and exited the track after it stopped. "So glad to see you and your tanks Hans. Where is the rest of the Brigade?" Asked Ansgar.

"Between here and home Mads, lots of enemy air making things tough" was Johansen's reply. "I was told to report to you from Brigade HQ, so here I am," Johansen explained.

"Great, let's get to work. I think the guys that just hit us are coming this way," Ansgar stated.

With Johansen's ten Leopard 1A3s, his force now had some firepower to stop the enemy's thrust. Ansgar also took stock of his own force. After sending the wounded back and moving around personnel he was down to two full troops, plus the attached TOWs, which up until now had been his only long range anti-tank. While he had solid infantry, they would have been left with defending themselves with their Carl Gustav and M72 LAW launchers versus the tanks at close range. The arrival of Johansen's Leopards was huge stroke of luck.

A West German Marder appeared on the road heading for Ansgar's command post. The APC stopped near Ansgar and Johansen and the rear doors opened with a West German *Hauptman* and his radio operator stepping out. "Where is your CO? The tall Panzergrenadier asked.

"Here" replied Ansgar. The *Hauptman* reached out his hand and introduced himself "*Hauptman* Joreg Freytag, 6th Panzergrenadier Division, glad to meet you, but I mean to speak with the commander of the Jutland Brigade".

"Well, he is it" Johansen sarcastically replied.

Freytag looked puzzled and asked, "I thought the whole brigade if not the whole division should be in place by now?"

"Well the Reds had other ideas. We have a large company sized battlegroup of tanks and mechanised infantry," Ansgar informed the Captain.

Freytag looked worried and explained "Most of the 6th Panzergrenadier Division is stuck fighting south of Lubeck, they got really torn apart by the main enemy attack. We were hoping you guys would be down to protect our left flank against any diversionary attacks to the northwest".

Ansgar felt almost insulted that the battle he had just fought was considered by his ally to be a "diversionary attack" however he did not know the trouble a that the 6th Panzergrenadier Division was in at the moment.

"We will do what we can. We do expect the brigade to arrive shortly. What can we expect from you guys as support" Ansgar asked the German.

"Not much, but we have a few batteries of guns deployed behind us, some AAA, and of course our *Luftwaffe* and helicopters" explained Freytag.

"We will take all the help we can get right now, thanks" replied Ansgar.

"I will leave my radio operator and my operations officer with you to coordinate fire support and anything you may need from us. *Leutnant* Lehmann, please stay with, oh I forgot to ask your name Herr Captain?" Freytag asked.

"Ansgar, Mads Ansgar, and thanks," Ansgar replied.

DUSK

The sun disappeared behind Ansgar's position and for a moment he thought he had caught a break. After being pushed back from his initial position Ansgar thought the Poles would exploit their success right away rather than risking a night fight. That hope was soon dashed as a report came in over his communication net.

"King Command, this is King 3, contact, enemy tanks, unknown type, headed west northwest via the road out of Schwochel, King 3 out".

Before he had time to process that event, the radio came to life again and this time it was *Premierløjtnant* Johansen "Command actual, this is Dragoon Actual, correction on the previous, enemy force made up of at least 12 BMPs, same position and direction as the last, out."

"Perhaps the Leos were able to see things clearer in their sights," mused Knudsen, trying to help his commander determine what was going on.

"Or perhaps we are dealing with two different forces, *Oversergent*," was Ansgar's friendly reply. Ansgar felt confident of what was in front of him. He expected the T-55 battalion to be the first to approach his position, with the motor infantry right behind. Usually the Pact leads with recce, however the first report from Kristoffersen said tanks, not the usual wheeled recce he would have expected. No matter what was in front of him, the enemy force was heading in the direction of Ahrensbök, right in between his forces, falling into another perfectly laid trap.

Before too long Ansgar got another report on his command net. "King Command this is King 2, confirm reports of King 3 and Dragoon Actual, out."

This report made the situation clearer to Ansgar and with that he lifted the hand set of his radio and gave his forces their orders, "King 2 and 3, Dragoon Actual, engage all targets, King Command out".

UNCERTAINTY

Somewhere out there was an enemy T-55 battalion that had yet to reveal itself, and that conserned Ansgar. Throughout his career Ansgar had prided himself on his good judgement and his refusal to make snap judgements. He was starting to feel that since he had not heard from any other units of the Jutland Division or the Germans, that his position may well be the extreme left flank of the NATO battle line in Germany.

As he analysed the situation, the truth was right in front of him. Ansgar knew he had been played. His feeling were reinforced as he saw heavy calibre shells explode in the positions of King 1 and 2. Ansgar looked at Knudsen, "This is not the main enemy attack, he is behind us. Contact all units and tell them to pull out via Ahrensbök to the cross roads of Autobahn 21 and route 430 at Bornhöved, ASAP!"

Knudsen quickly replied, "But sir, that is 35 kilometres away, well behind our planned line…"

Ansgar cut him off quickly, "I know, but it's the only place we can stop them, trust me on this." With a nod, Knudsen relayed the message to all of the commands units.

ERIKSEN'S LEOPARD PLATOON

"Did you hear that?" Lt Eriksen asked his crew. The leader of 'Dragoon 1' knew from the sounds he was hearing to the south that a pitched battle was going on, and from the order to reposition things were not going well. "Okey, let's get out of here" Eriksen said on his platoon's comm net. He knew from the plan put in place that he was to cover the north flank of the battalion as they pulled back.

"Platoon, follow me," and Eriksen's Leopard 1 roared to life and the other two tanks would follow. Knowing that on his left flank were friendly units Eriksen gave the order on the platoon net, "Cover right," and with that all three of the Leopard turrets swung to the right, ready to engage any targets that appear on that flank.

As Eriksen's Leopards were racing through the dark, the gunner in Eriksen's lead tank started to see some unusual blobs on his IR screen. These blobs grew more familiar as the range closed and the gunner finally spoke out, "Sir, I think we have company to our right."

Eriksen looked and saw what the gunner saw: a long line of T-55s on the road to Ahrensbök. Eriksen knew that he had to act, and act quickly, "Dragoon 1 halt, open fire!"

The first shots from his platoon were on their way. These were wild and missed their marks. The near hits were enough to stop the enemy column as they too learned that they were not alone. Eriksen got on his command net and contacted Captain Johansen, "Enemy tanks are south of Route 432, sir, more than twenty of them. We are engaging them."

The reply was grim and telling. "You have to hold them, we are retreating through the town now. We will let you know when we are clear."

Eriksen then turned his attention to the formation in front of him. At least two T-55s were burning, and the rest were turning towards his small platoon and starting to return fire.

"Keep up the fire and movement Dragoon 1," Eriksen told his platoon. Just as he transmitted that message, Platoon Sergeant Madsen's tank blew up, lifting the tank off the ground and knocking its turret off. The blast jarred Eriksen and his crew. Stunned, but still in command of his faculties, Eriksen yelled at his crew, "Keep moving and firing or we are next."

Things were desperate, and he urgently radioed Captain Johansen, "Sir, Dragoon 1 is down to two tanks, one destroyed, at least four enemy tanks burning. What is your status?"

Johansen replied, "Dragoon 2 is in the rear of the column. We are almost out of Ahrensbök. Suggest you disengage and join our rear."

"Copy," was Eriksen quick reply.

The lead Polish T-55s moved ahead, slowly passing the burning Danish Leopard 1, before picking up speed.

"Dragoon 1-3 take the lead, head into the town and rejoin Dragoon 2, I'm right behind you," radioed Eriksen. The two Leopards picked up speed and he could see Dragoon 1-3 reach the outskirts of town. His tank, Dragoon 1-1, was right behind them.

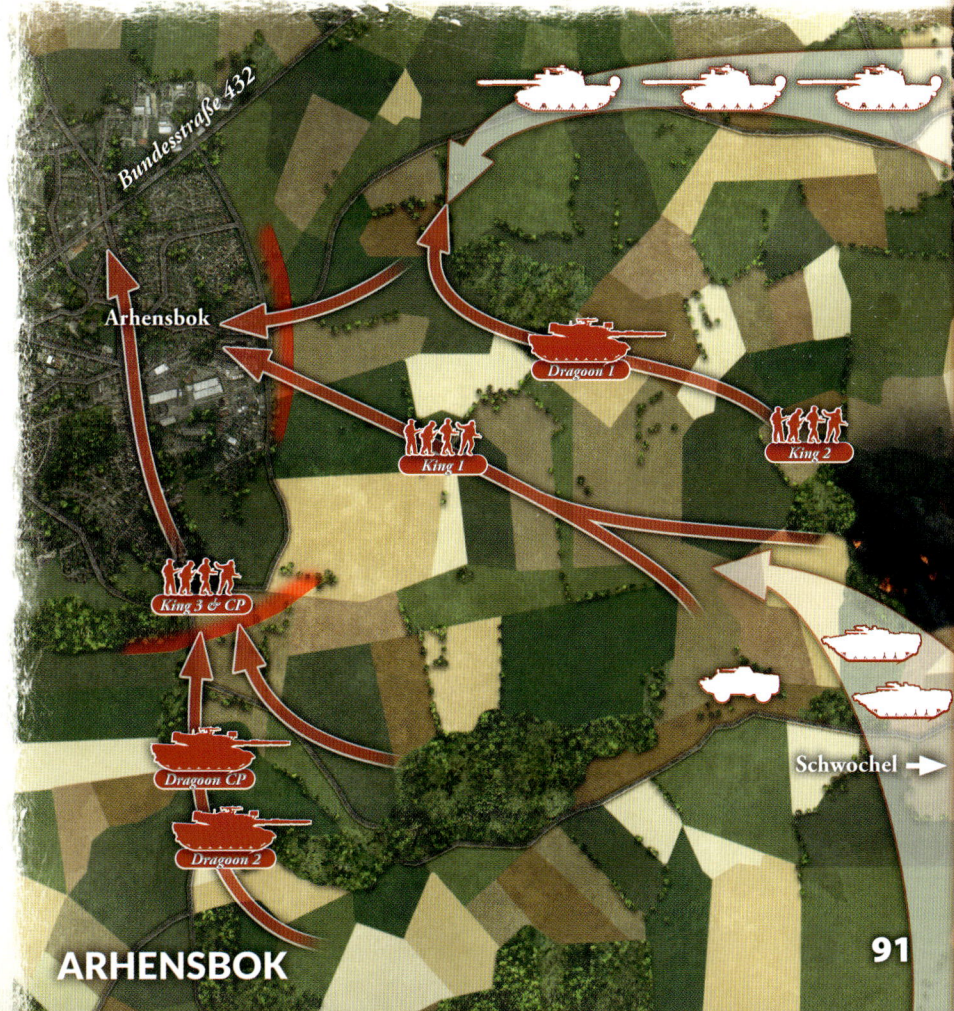

ARHENSBOK

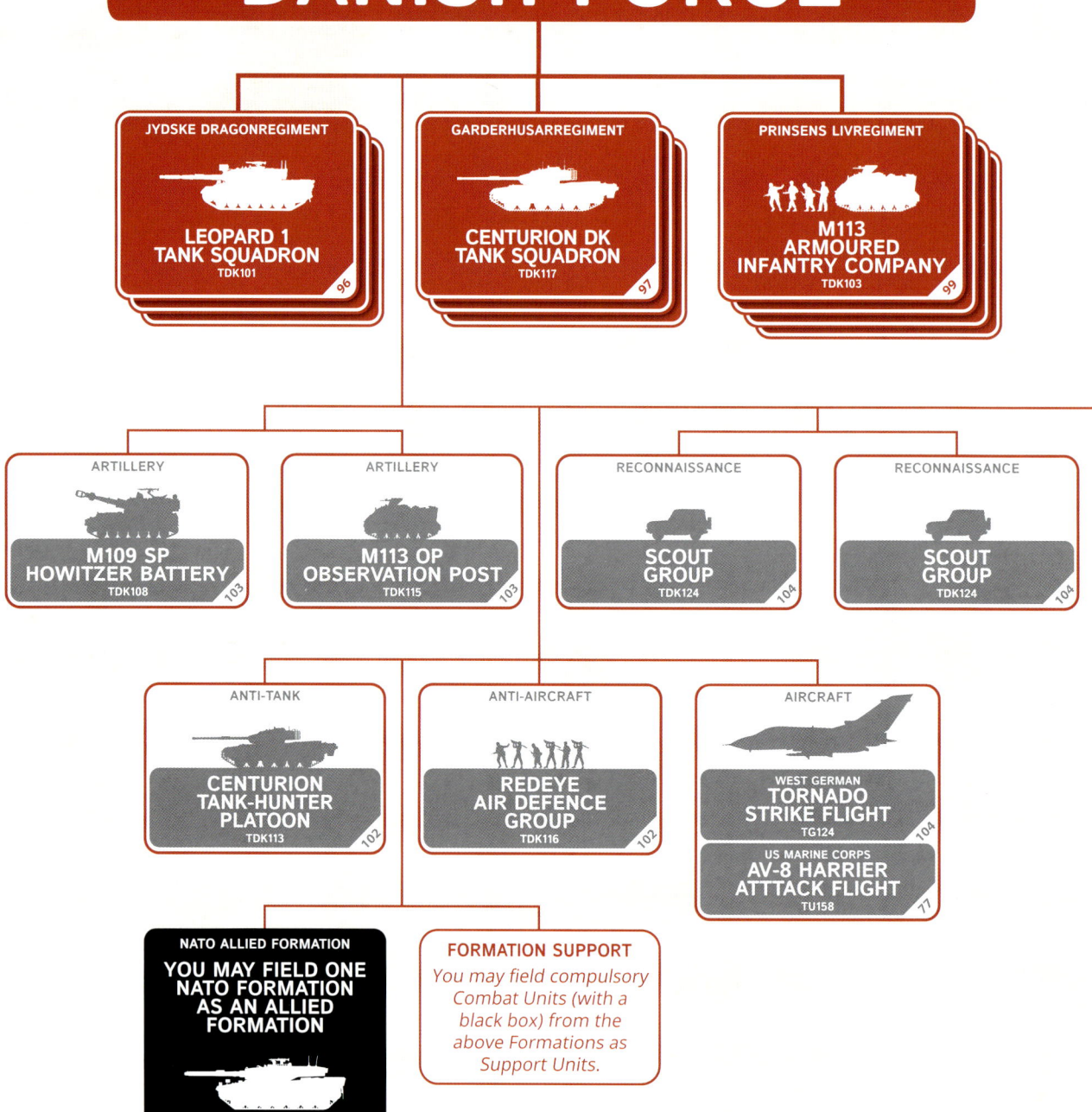

DANISH SPECIAL RULES

The Danish Army has a number of features and weapons. These are reflected in the following special rules.

ACCURATE

The Centurion Mk V tanks used by the Danish tank-hunting units are fitted with a co-ax .50 cal (12.7mm) machine-gun for ranging the 20 pdr (84mm) main gun.

> If stationary, a Weapon with Accurate has no To Hit penalty for shooting at ranges over 16"/40cm.

BAZOOKA SKIRTS

Leopard 1 tanks are fitted with 'bazooka skirts', spaced armour to protect them from light, hand-held anti-tank weapons.

> Teams with Bazooka Skirts have Front and Side armour rating of 10 against HEAT weapons.

NATO ALLIED SUPPORT

Often divisions from other NATO nations, such as West German 6th Panzergrenadier Division in LANDJUT, fought alongside Danish forces.

A NATO Allied Formation can be from any other Force with a NATO Allied Formation in its support.

You can take an Allied Formation or Units as part of your Force. An Allied Formation or Unit obeys all the rules for its own nationality. An Allied Formation Commander can only join Units in its own Formation or nationality and only its Formation or nationality Units can benefit from its Command Leadership (see page 25 and 64 of the rulebook).

An Allied Formation does not count as a Formation when counting how many Formations are left when determining if you have lost the game (see page 65 of the rulebook).

Rules for West German Formations and Units are found in the pages marked in WWIII-05 World War III: West German.

DANISH TANK SQUADRONS

Kaptajn Martin Hansen leaned back into the seat of his Leopard 1, grimacing. These Soviet Naval troops he had been engaging since first light just wouldn't back down. His squadron normally comprised his command Leopard 1 tank and three troops each of three Leopard 1 tanks, but today he had instead exchanged a Leopard troop for a platoon from the third company of the battalion, an M113 mounted infantry platoon. These foot-sloggers were invaluable in the marshy terrain of the Jutland coastline.

The Squadron had been recalled urgently with warnings from headquarters that naval forces were incoming. This was every Dane's nightmare – an attack upon home soil. Everyone was saying this was an ødelægge, a screwup of the worst kind. After rushing to find his crews at short notice, they had found that some of their precious Leopards were not ready to roll out. Scheduled maintenance? Really? He shook his head at the frustrations.

Ever since arriving at the shore, Hansen had bitten his lip with frustration. Waves of BTR-60 amphibious APCs were rolling in from landing ships in the shallows. Already he was running low on the precious ammunition being devoured by his main gun. Having lost count after the first dozen APCs, he started sweating as he realised that the Soviets were now bringing in some enormous hovercraft, each carrying three T-55 tanks and rapidly making their way to the sand.

"Gunner, HEAT, engage giant hovercraft at eleven o'clock, four hundred metres! Fire when ready."

Hansen's gunner, Overkonstabel Thor Rasmussen, glanced up at the boss. Did he really hear that command? APCs sure, they did not scare him when they fired back. Tanks, he could live with shooting, but how much hope did he have against a naval target? Then he realised how fast the target was closing. At a speed of 100 kilometres an hour, he had to be fast although the target was massive.

"Did you hear me, Thor? Fire," rasped Hansen, the fumes making his voice sound more angry than he felt. Fatigue was creeping in.

"On the way!" Yelled Rasmussen.

Satisfyingly, the outgoing round smashed its way explosively through the front skirting of the behemoth. The Soviet Zubr hovercraft slid sideways, scattering BTR60s swimming nearby as it churned the waters, sinking fast.

With no time to gloat over his victory, Hansen laughingly shoved the dumbstruck gunner and exhorted him to keep firing.

LEOPARD 1 TANK SQUADRONS

All the tank squadrons of the *Jyske Dragonregiment* (Jutland Dragoon Regiment), the *Prinsens Livregiment* (The Prince's Life Regiment), the *Dronnings Livregiment* (Queen's Life Regiment), the *Fynske Livregiment* (Funen Life Regiment), and the *Kongens Jyske Fodregiment* (The King's Jutland Foot Regiment) were equipped with the Leopard 1A3.

A Danish *Kampvognseskadron* (tank squadron) has a total of ten tanks, one Company Commander's tank and three platoons of three tanks each. Each squadron also had an entourage of support and resupply vehicles and personnel. The tank squadrons were the formations in the Danish army with the highest ratio of professionals to conscripts, due to the skill level required to operate and maintain the weapon systems of the squadrons. Squadrons would often be attached to an infantry company or have infantry attached to it in operations. The squadrons would be the highly mobile armoured fire-support when operating in support of infantry, providing anti-tank capabilities and optics generally exceeding those of the infantry platoons. The squadron would utilise their speed and accurate weapons, to engage the enemy from afar and then reposition.

CENTURION TANK SQUADRONS

From 1985 the tank squadrons of the *Sjællandske Livregiment* (Zealand Life Regiment), the *Danske Livregiment* (Danish Life Regiment), the *Gardehusarregimentet* (The Guard Hussar Regiment), and the *Den Kongelige Livgarden* (The Royal Life Guards) were equipped with upgraded Centurion DK tanks.

A Centurion *Kampvognseskadron* (Tank squadron) was organised like their Jutland counterparts, with one Commander's tank and three platoons of three, for a total of ten tanks. Like the Jutland squadrons, the Zealand (*Sjælland*) squadrons also sported a higher ratio of professionals to conscripts than other formations in the Danish army.

The Centurions lacked the speed of the Leopards, but this was considered less critical due to the main operating area, the islands of Zealand, Lolland and Falster. The distances that needed to be covered were considerably shorter than that of the Jutland brigades.

HÆREN
LEOPARD 1 TANK SQUADRON

You must field the Formation HQ and one Combat Unit from each black box.
You may also field one Combat Unit from each grey box.

LEOPARD 1 TANK SQUADRON HQ
TDK101

1x Leopard 1 — **3 POINTS**

• TANK FORMATION • BAZOOKA SKIRTS • THERMAL IMAGING •

COURAGE 3+	SKILL 3+
MORALE 3+	ASSAULT 4+
REMOUNT 3+	COUNTERATTACK 3+

IS HIT ON 4+

FRONT	SIDE	TOP
9	5	1

TACTICAL	TERRAIN DASH	CROSS COUNTRY DASH	ROAD DASH	CROSS
10"/25CM	16"/40CM	28"/70CM	32"/80CM	2+

WEAPON	RANGE	ROF HALTED	ROF MOVING	ANTI-TANK	FIRE-POWER	NOTES
105mm L7 gun	40"/100CM	2	2	19	2+	Laser Rangefinder, Smoke, Stabiliser
7.62mm AA MG	16"/40CM	3	3	2	6	
7.62mm MG	16"/40CM	1	1	2	6	

ARMOUR — LEOPARD 1 TANK PLATOON — TDK102 (96)

ARMOUR — LEOPARD 1 TANK PLATOON — TDK102 (96)

INFANTRY — M113 ARMOURED INFANTRY PLATOON — TDK104 (100)

ANTI-TANK — M113 TOW PLATOON — TDK107 (101)

ARMOUR — LEOPARD 1 TANK PLATOON — TDK102 (96)

ARTILLERY — M106 120MM MORTAR PLATOON — TDK106 (101)

ARTILLERY — M109 SP HOWITZER BATTERY — TDK108 (103)

You may field a Combat Unit from a black box as a Support Unit for your Force.

HÆREN
LEOPARD 1 TANK PLATOON

LEOPARD 1 TANK PLATOON

3x Leopard 1 — **10 POINTS**

• TANK UNIT • BAZOOKA SKIRTS • THERMAL IMAGING •

COURAGE 4+	SKILL 4+
MORALE 4+	ASSAULT 4+
REMOUNT 3+	COUNTERATTACK 4+

IS HIT ON 4+

FRONT	SIDE	TOP
9	5	1

TACTICAL	TERRAIN DASH	CROSS COUNTRY DASH	ROAD DASH	CROSS
10"/25CM	16"/40CM	28"/70CM	32"/80CM	2+

WEAPON	RANGE	ROF HALTED	ROF MOVING	ANTI-TANK	FIRE-POWER	NOTES
105mm L7 gun	40"/100CM	2	2	19	2+	Laser Rangefinder, Smoke, Stabiliser
7.62mm AA MG	16"/40CM	3	3	2	6	
7.62mm MG	16"/40CM	1	1	2	6	

The Leopard 1A3 entered service with the Danish Army *(Hæren)*, replacing the Centurion in front line service with the Jutland brigades. Between 1976 and 1978 all the Jutland *(Jylland)* tank squadrons were equipped with the new tank. The Leopard 1 was chosen over the Centurion for its increased speed and manoeuvrability, which could be better utilised when changing from one firing position to the next, especially in the relatively flat terrain of the North German plain and the Jutland Peninsula. Another consideration was that the Leopard 1 was used by the West German *Bundeswehr*, with which the Jutland brigades would cooperate if war broke out, allowing them to share supply and logistics.

CENTURION DK TANK SQUADRON
HÆREN

You must field the Formation HQ and one Combat Unit from each black box.
You may also field one Combat Unit from each grey box.

• TANK FORMATION • BAZOOKA SKIRTS • INFRA-RED (IR) •

CENTURION DK TANK SQUADRON HQ — TDK117
1x Centurion DK — **3 POINTS**

COURAGE 3+	SKILL 3+
MORALE 3+	ASSAULT 4+
REMOUNT 3+	COUNTERATTACK 3+

IS HIT ON 4+
FRONT 13 — SIDE 6 — TOP 2

TACTICAL	TERRAIN DASH	CROSS COUNTRY DASH	ROAD DASH	CROSS
10"/25cm	12"/30cm	16"/40cm	16"/40cm	2+

WEAPON	RANGE	ROF HALTED	ROF MOVING	ANTI-TANK	FIRE-POWER	NOTES
105mm L7 gun	40"/100cm	2	1	19	2+	Laser Rangefinder, Smoke, Stabiliser
7.62mm MG	16"/40cm	3	3	2	6	

ARMOUR — CENTURION DK TANK PLATOON TDK114 (97)
ARMOUR — CENTURION DK TANK PLATOON TDK114 (97)
ARMOUR — CENTURION DK TANK PLATOON TDK114 (97)
INFANTRY — M113 ARMOURED INFANTRY PLATOON TDK104 (100)
ANTI-TANK — M113 TOW PLATOON TDK107 (101)
ARTILLERY — M106 120mm MORTAR PLATOON TDK106 (101)
ARTILLERY — M109 SP HOWITZER BATTERY TDK108 (103)

You may field a Combat Unit from a black box as a Support Unit for your Force.

CENTURION DK TANK PLATOON
HÆREN

CENTURION DK TANK PLATOON
3x Centurion DK — **8 POINTS**

• TANK UNIT • BAZOOKA SKIRTS • INFRA-RED (IR) •

COURAGE 4+	SKILL 4+
MORALE 4+	ASSAULT 4+
REMOUNT 3+	COUNTERATTACK 4+

IS HIT ON 4+
FRONT 13 — SIDE 6 — TOP 2

Originally delivered to Denmark in 1953 and paid for by the US, before half of the fleet was upgunned in the 1960s with the 105mm L7. Between 1982 and 1985 the ageing Centurion tanks received the DK upgrade package that increased their night fighting capabilities with a PZB-200 camera, the same as the one used on the Leopard 1 tanks, a laser rangefinder and a primitive thermal sighting system, known as a thermal tracer. With the new designation as Centurion Mk V, 2 DK, usually called Centurion DK for short, they served for the remainder of the Cold War with the Zealand (Sjælland) brigades.

TACTICAL	TERRAIN DASH	CROSS COUNTRY DASH	ROAD DASH	CROSS
10"/25cm	12"/30cm	16"/40cm	16"/40cm	2+

WEAPON	RANGE	ROF HALTED	ROF MOVING	ANTI-TANK	FIRE-POWER	NOTES
105mm L7 gun	40"/100cm	2	1	19	2+	Laser Rangefinder, Smoke, Stabiliser
7.62mm MG	16"/40cm	3	3	2	6	

Crew: 4 - commander, gunner, loader, driver
Weight: 51 tonnes
Length: 9.75m (31' 8")
Width: 3.40 (11')
Height: 3.22m (10' 5")
Armour: 51-152mm RHA
Weapons: 105mm Royal Ordnance L7A1 L/52 rifled Gun
1x MG3 7.62mm MG
Speed: 35 km/h (22 mph)
Engine: V12-cylinder Rolls-Royce Meteor Mk IV B.
650 hp (485 kW)
Range: 100 km (62 miles)

ARMOURED INFANTRY COMPANY

AKM rounds spattered the facade of the bar, scattering fragments of beer posters and splintering glass in equal measures. Larssen's platoon sergeant instinctively ducked at the latest round of fire.

"Damn Polish Marines won't take no for an answer, sir"

Jens Larssen grimaced at the forced humour, rapidly thinking through how to push back the Warpac Naval Landing Forces currently tying up his small force. Since the Poles had arrived with their Soviet Allies, it had been gruelling fighting house-to-house, barely giving a metre of ground.

"Madsen, get your Carl Gustav up here. Niklaus, yours too. Get your butts moving, need this yesterday!"

Each team of two tank hunters appeared as if from nowhere, one of each lugging the 14 kg manpacked anti-tank weapon while the other strained with extra ammunition. Exhausted from scrambling upstairs in the ruined bar, the four men peered expectantly at their platoon commander.

"Right, here's how we are going to sort this. Madsen, Niklaus, you each are to load with splintex on my command. Get ready to spray the street below and shift those Polish sailor boys. Christensen, get the APCs ready at the back door. I expect once we have their attention, they can pinpoint the windows we are firing from, we are going to need to get out of here quickly."

Furious nods all round from the grubby faces of the Danish Livregiment troops showed their faith in their leader's advice. Løjtnant Larssen had kept them alive for the past day and a half and they had high hopes he would continue to do so.

On a hoarsely barked count of three, the two Carl Gustav teams sighted their weapons. At a count of two, they hovered their fingers over the firing mechanism. On the command of one, they simultaneously unleashed a hail of arrows from the canisters in their Carl Gustav recoilless rifles.

Screams of anguish and shock filtered through the smoke and ruin of the street. Clearly some unlucky enemy had been in the wrong place at the wrong time.

"That's it, boys, hoof it back to the Tracks." Outside could be heard the roar of the three M113s' diesel engines revving in the cold morning, preparing to re-embark their precious cargo.

"Goodbye Rødvig, we did our best, hope to see you again soon..."
whispered Larssen reverently as he left the building.

The *Panserinfanterikompagni* (Armoured Infantry Company) formed the core of the Danish Army from 1964, when the first batch of M113s entered Danish service. The company was made up of a command section with one M113 transport and three platoons of infantry with M113 transports. Furthermore, the infantry company had a mortar section of two M125 mortar carriers, that in some companies was replaced by M106 mortar carriers. Finally, it also had a section of M113 TOW vehicles.

The infantry company would often have tanks attached to it or have platoons attached to a tank squadron in operations. Defensively the infantry would act as either a screening force for the tanks or as a defensive hard point. Offensively the infantry would act as an assault and clearance force, clearing out woods, towns and assaulting enemy positions.

M113 ARMOURED INFANTRY COMPANY
HÆREN

You must field the Formation HQ and one Combat Unit from each black box.
You may also field one Combat Unit from each grey box.

M113 ARMOURED INFANTRY COMPANY HQ (TDK103)

- 1x G3 rifle team
- 1x M113 (TDK109)

1 POINT

• INFANTRY FORMATION • HQ TRANSPORT •

COURAGE 3+	SKILL 3+
MORALE 3+	ASSAULT 4+
RALLY 3+	COUNTERATTACK 3+

IS HIT ON	INFANTRY SAVE
4+	3+

TACTICAL	TERRAIN DASH	CROSS COUNTRY DASH	ROAD DASH	CROSS
8"/20cm	8"/20cm	12"/30cm	12"/30cm	AUTO

WEAPON	RANGE	ROF HALTED	ROF MOVING	ANTI-TANK	FIRE-POWER	NOTES
G3 rifle team	16"/40cm	1	1	2	6	

INFANTRY — M113 ARMOURED INFANTRY PLATOON (TDK104) — 100

INFANTRY — M113 ARMOURED INFANTRY PLATOON (TDK104) — 100

ARMOUR — LEOPARD 1 TANK PLATOON (TDK102) — 96 / CENTURION DK TANK PLATOON (TDK114) — 97

ANTI-TANK — M113 TOW PLATOON (TDK107) — 101

INFANTRY — M113 ARMOURED INFANTRY PLATOON (TDK104) — 100

ARTILLERY — M125 81MM MORTAR PLATOON (TDK105) — 101

ARTILLERY — M106 120MM MORTAR PLATOON (TDK106) — 101

ARTILLERY — M109 SP HOWITZER BATTERY (TDK108) — 103

You may field a Combat Unit from a black box as a Support Unit for your Force.

M113 ARMOURED INFANTRY PLATOON
HÆREN

M113 ARMOURED INFANTRY PLATOON	
3x MG3 team with M72 LAW anti-tank	
3x Carl Gustav anti-tank team	
3x M113 (TDK109)	**5 POINTS**
2x MG3 team with M72 LAW anti-tank	
2x Carl Gustav anti-tank team	
2x M113 (TDK109)	**3 POINTS**

A Danish *Panserinfanteri Deling* (Armoured Infantry Platoon) was generally made up of three groups, each in turn was made up of around nine to eleven soldiers lead by a sergeant. Each group was armed with one M/62 (MG3) machine-gun, one M/79 (Carl Gustav) recoilless rifle, M/72 LAWs and M/75 (G-3) semi-automatic rifles.

The *Panserinfanteri Deling* had three crewed M113s armed with .50 cal machine-guns, one for each group, to transport the platoon to and from the battlefield. In defensive operations the M113s, with their heavy machines-guns, could act as machine-gun nests giving supporting defensive fire, and in offensive operations as a base of fire for the assaulting infantry.

Crew: 3 - commander, gunner, driver + 7 passengers
Weight: 28.2 tonnes
Length: 6.79m (22' 3")
Width: 3.24m (10' 8")
Height: 2.95m (9' 9")
Armour: Welded steel 30mm
Weapons: Rheinmetall 20mm Rh 202 Gun 1x .50 cal AA MG
Speed: 75 km/h (47 mph)
Engine: MB 833 Ea-500 V6 turbo diesel engine, 600 hp (447 kW)
Range: 520 km (323 miles)

• INFANTRY UNIT •

COURAGE 4+	SKILL 4+
MORALE 4+	ASSAULT 4+
RALLY 4+	COUNTERATTACK 4+

IS HIT ON	INFANTRY SAVE
4+	3+

TACTICAL	TERRAIN DASH	CROSS COUNTRY DASH	ROAD DASH	CROSS
8"/20CM	8"/20CM	12"/30CM	12"/30CM	AUTO

WEAPON	RANGE	ROF HALTED	ROF MOVING	ANTI-TANK	FIRE-POWER	NOTES
MG3 team or	16"/40CM	3	2	2	5+	
M72 LAW anti-tank	12"/30CM	1	1	12	5+	HEAT, Slow Firing
Carl Gustav anti-tank team	16"/40CM	1	1	17	3+	HEAT, Slow Firing

M113 TRANSPORT
HÆREN

• TANK ATTACHMENT • AMPHIBIOUS • PASSENGERS 3 •

COURAGE 4+	SKILL 4+
MORALE 4+	ASSAULT 5+
REMOUNT 4+	COUNTERATTACK 5+

IS HIT ON 4+		
FRONT	SIDE	TOP
3	2	1

TACTICAL	TERRAIN DASH	CROSS COUNTRY DASH	ROAD DASH	CROSS
10"/25CM	16"/40CM	24"/60CM	32"/80CM	3+

WEAPON	RANGE	ROF HALTED	ROF MOVING	ANTI-TANK	FIRE-POWER
.50 cal AA MG	20"/50CM	3	2	4	5+

HÆREN
M125 81MM MORTAR PLATOON

M125 81MM MORTAR PLATOON	
2x M125 81mm	**1 POINT**

The Danish Army fields a total of 56 M113 based mortar carriers. These are a mix of M106 and M125. The M125 is armed with a 81mm mortar. The vehicle carries 120 81mm mortar rounds in side-mounted racks. Additionally the vehicle is armoured with a M2 12.7mm (.50 cal) heavy machine-gun.

• TANK UNIT • AMPHIBIOUS •

COURAGE 4+	SKILL 4+
MORALE 4+	ASSAULT 6
REMOUNT 4+	COUNTERATTACK 6

IS HIT ON 4+		
FRONT	SIDE	TOP
3	2	0

TACTICAL	TERRAIN DASH	CROSS COUNTRY DASH	ROAD DASH	CROSS
10"/25CM	16"/40CM	24"/60CM	32"/80CM	3+

WEAPON	RANGE	ROF HALTED	ROF MOVING	ANTI-TANK	FIRE-POWER	NOTES
81mm mortar	56"/140CM	ARTILLERY		1	4+	Smoke Bombardment
.50cal AA MG	20"/50CM	3	2	4	5+	

HÆREN
M106 120MM MORTAR PLATOON

M106 120MM MORTAR PLATOON	
4x M106 120mm	**4 POINTS**
2x M106 120mm	**2 POINTS**

Following the West German example, the Danish have rearmed their M106 mortar carriers with the Tampella 120mm mortar. This weapon replaces the American 4.2"/107mm M30 mortar. The modified M106 can carry 63 120mm mortar rounds.

• TANK UNIT • AMPHIBIOUS •

COURAGE 4+	SKILL 4+
MORALE 4+	ASSAULT 6
REMOUNT 4+	COUNTERATTACK 6

IS HIT ON 4+		
FRONT	SIDE	TOP
3	2	0

TACTICAL	TERRAIN DASH	CROSS COUNTRY DASH	ROAD DASH	CROSS
10"/25CM	16"/40CM	24"/60CM	32"/80CM	3+

WEAPON	RANGE	ROF HALTED	ROF MOVING	ANTI-TANK	FIRE-POWER	NOTES
120mm mortar	64"/160CM	ARTILLERY		3	3+	Smoke Bombardment
.50 cal AA MG	20"/50CM	3	2	4	5+	

Crew: 5 - commander, gunner, 2x loader, driver
Weight: 12.5 tonnes
Length: 5.12m (16' 9.5")
Width: 2.69m (8' 10")
Height: 2.64m (8' 8")
Armour: 38mm Aluminium
Weapons: Rheinmetall/Tampella M120 120mm mortar
1x .50 cal AA MG
Speed: 62 km/h (38 mph)
Engine: Detroit Diesel V6, 210 hp (154 kw)
Range: 550 km (340 miles)

HÆREN
M113 TOW PLATOON

M113 TOW PLATOON	
4x M113 TOW	**6 POINTS**
2x M113 TOW	**3 POINTS**

The Danes have fitted 56 M113 with the TOW launcher (this variant is sometimes known as a M150). Each vehicle carries ten Improved TOW missiles. The launcher has gone through several upgrades and is equipped with thermal sights. Effective range of the Improved TOW is between 65 and 3700 metres. The vehicles were also armed with a M2 12.7mm (.50 cal) machine-gun.

• TANK UNIT • AMPHIBIOUS • THERMAL IMAGING •

COURAGE 4+	SKILL 4+
MORALE 4+	ASSAULT 5+
REMOUNT 4+	COUNTERATTACK 5+

IS HIT ON 4+		
FRONT	SIDE	TOP
3	2	0

TACTICAL	TERRAIN DASH	CROSS COUNTRY DASH	ROAD DASH	CROSS
10"/25CM	16"/40CM	24"/60CM	32"/80CM	3+

WEAPON	RANGE	ROF HALTED	ROF MOVING	ANTI-TANK	FIRE-POWER	NOTES
Improved TOW missile	8"/20CM - 48"/120CM	1	-	21	3+	Guided, HEAT
.50 cal AA MG	20"/50CM	3	2	4	5+	

DANISH SUPPORT UNITS

HÆREN
CENTURION TANK-HUNTER PLATOON

CENTURION TANK-HUNTER PLATOON	
3x Centurion	**5 POINTS**

The *Panserjagerdeling* (Tank-hunter Platoon) was equipped with the older Centurion tank, which were mostly the Centurion Mk V armed with the 20 pdr (84mm) gun. They were manned primarily by Reserve personnel, which would be mobilised in the case of an imminent conflict. Even though the ageing Centurion was retired from front line service in the Jutland armoured squadrons, it was still pressed into service, in a defensive role, where it would mostly have assisted infantry, in prepared defensive positions. For this purpose, the 20 pdr gun was considered adequate.

• TANK UNIT • BAZOOKA SKIRTS •

COURAGE 4+	SKILL 4+
MORALE 4+	ASSAULT 4+
REMOUNT 3+	COUNTERATTACK 4+

IS HIT ON 4+
FRONT 13 | SIDE 6 | TOP 2

TACTICAL	TERRAIN DASH	CROSS COUNTRY DASH	ROAD DASH	CROSS
10"/25CM	12"/30CM	16"/40CM	16"/40CM	2+

WEAPON	RANGE	ROF HALTED	ROF MOVING	ANTI-TANK	FIRE-POWER	NOTES
OQF 20 pdr gun	40"/100CM	2	1	17	2+	Accurate, Smoke, Stabiliser
.50 cal Spotting MG	20"/50CM	1	1	4	5+	Slow Firing
7.62mm MG	16"/40CM	3	3	2	6	

Crew: 4 – commander, gunner, loader, driver
Weight: 51 tonnes
Length: 9.75m (31' 8")
Width: 3.40 (11')
Height: 3.22m (10' 5")
Armour: 51-152mm RHA

Weapons: Ordnance QF 20 pdr (84mm) L/67 rifled Gun
1x MG3 7.62mm MG
Speed: 35 km/h (22 mph)
Engine: V12-cylinder Rolls-Royce Meteor Mk IV B.
650 hp (485 kW)

HÆREN
REDEYE AIR DEFENCE GROUP

REDEYE AIR DEFENCE GROUP	
4x Redeye AA missile team 2x M113 (TDK109)	**4 POINTS**
2x Redeye AA missile team 1x M113 (TDK109)	**2 POINTS**

The Air Defense Battalion's *Luftværnsgrupper* (Air Defense Groups) are mounted in M113s. These were assigned to specific sectors of the area of operations or could be assigned to companies, depending on needs. Divisionally the Air Defense battalion had a mobile radar, and a mobile communications centre. These were used to radio the relevant air defense groups from the HQ, if anything appeared on the radar.

• INFANTRY UNIT • HEAVY WEAPON •

COURAGE 4+	SKILL 4+
MORALE 4+	ASSAULT 4+
RALLY 4+	COUNTERATTACK 4+

IS HIT ON	INFANTRY SAVE
4+	3+

TACTICAL	TERRAIN DASH	CROSS COUNTRY DASH	ROAD DASH	CROSS
8"/20CM	8"/20CM	12"/30CM	12"/30CM	AUTO

WEAPON	RANGE	ROF HALTED	ROF MOVING	ANTI-TANK	FIRE-POWER	NOTES
Redeye AA missile team	48"/120CM	3	–	–	5+	Guided AA.

Due to the lack of any SPAAG systems in the Danish Army, a total reliance was placed on stationary AA emplacements, MANPADs and the Royal Danish Air Force for air defense. The radio communications between the Air Defense Battalion and its groups was considered so vital that they were often exempt from general radio silence orders.

M109 SP HOWITZER BATTERY
HÆREN

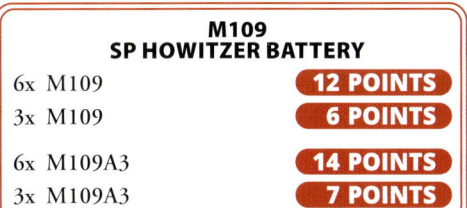

M109 SP HOWITZER BATTERY	
6x M109	12 POINTS
3x M109	6 POINTS
6x M109A3	14 POINTS
3x M109A3	7 POINTS

The M109 self-propelled howitzer (*selvkørende haubits*) entered service with the artillery regiments of the Royal Danish Army in 1964, the same time the M113 entered service with the infantry.

The M109s are organised into two batteries of six SP howitzers, with each artillery battalion having three batteries. From 1985, the M109s began being upgraded to the M109A3 standard (M185 155mm long barrel howitzer) by the Danish Material Command. Additionally, the M109s were armed with a commander's hatch mounted 12.7mm (.50 cal) machine-gun.

• TANK UNIT •

COURAGE 4+	SKILL 4+
MORALE 4+	ASSAULT 5+
REMOUNT 4+	COUNTERATTACK 5+

IS HIT ON 4+

FRONT	SIDE	TOP
2	2	1

TACTICAL	TERRAIN DASH	CROSS COUNTRY DASH	ROAD DASH	CROSS
10"/25CM	16"/40CM	24"/60CM	28"/70CM	3+

WEAPON	RANGE	ROF HALTED	ROF MOVING	ANTI-TANK	FIRE-POWER	NOTES
M109 155mm howitzer	88"/220CM	ARTILLERY		4	2+	Smoke Bombardment
or Direct fire	24"/60CM	1	1	12	1+	Brutal, Slow Firing, Smoke
M109A3 155mm howitzer	96"/240CM	ARTILLERY		4	2+	Smoke Bombardment
or Direct fire	36"/90CM	1	1	15	1+	Brutal, Slow Firing, Smoke
.50 cal AA MG	20"/50CM	3	2	4	5+	

M113 OP OBSERVATION POST
HÆREN

M113 OP OBSERVATION POST	
1x M113 OP	1 POINT

You must field:
- *a M106 120mm Mortar Platoon* (TDK106), *or*
- *a M109 SP Howitzer Battery* (TDK108)
before you may field a M113 OP.

The forward observers of the Danish artillery are mounted in M113 carriers to provide them protection and mobility, as well as providing them room for their observation and communications equipment.

• INDEPENDENT TANK UNIT • AMPHIBIOUS • INFRA-RED (IR) • OBSERVER • SCOUT •

COURAGE 4+	SKILL 4+
MORALE 4+	ASSAULT 5+
REMOUNT 4+	COUNTERATTACK 5+

IS HIT ON 4+

FRONT	SIDE	TOP
3	2	1

TACTICAL	TERRAIN DASH	CROSS COUNTRY DASH	ROAD DASH	CROSS
10"/25CM	16"/40CM	24"/60CM	32"/80CM	3+

WEAPON	RANGE	ROF HALTED	ROF MOVING	ANTI-TANK	FIRE-POWER	NOTES
7.62mm AA MG	16"/40CM	3	3	2	6	

DANISH SUPPORT UNITS

HÆREN
SCOUT GROUP

SCOUT GROUP	
4x Mercedes jeep	3 POINTS

The Danes used a variety of light utility vehicles in the light reconnaissance role as well as various other utility roles. By 1985 the Danes had over 1300 Mercedes 240 G/24 light reconnaissance cars. A *Spejdersektion* (Scout Section) consists of four vehicles with a MG3 machine-gun each. Each vehicle has a crew of three who carry some M72 LAWs for anti-tank defence as well as their G3 battle rifles.

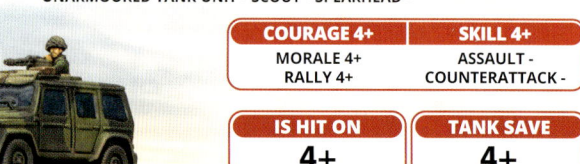

• UNARMOURED TANK UNIT • SCOUT • SPEARHEAD •

COURAGE 4+	SKILL 4+
MORALE 4+	ASSAULT -
RALLY 4+	COUNTERATTACK -

IS HIT ON	TANK SAVE
4+	4+

TACTICAL	TERRAIN DASH	CROSS COUNTRY DASH	ROAD DASH	CROSS
10"/25CM	12"/30CM	20"/50CM	48"/120CM	4+

WEAPON	RANGE	ROF HALTED	ROF MOVING	ANTI-TANK	FIRE-POWER	NOTES
M72 LAW anti-tank	12"/30CM	1	1	12	5+	HEAT, Slow Firing
7.62mm AA MG	16"/40CM	3	3	2	6	

WEST GERMAN LUFTWAFFE
TORNADO STRIKE FLIGHT

TORNADO STRIKE FLIGHT	
4x Tornado	8 POINTS
2x Tornado	4 POINTS

The Tornado strike-aircraft was developed as a joint project between Germany, Britain, and Italy.

The main role of the Tornado is as an Interdictor Strike (IDS) aircraft. The Tornado has a variable sweep-wing system. The pilot can change the sweep of the wings to change the aerodynamics of the aircraft. With the wings swept back drag was reduced during critical high-speed low-level dashes towards enemy positions. With the wings swept forward the Tornado takes on the characteristics of slower flight, allowing it to land and take-off on short runways. Low level flight is further enhanced by an innovative automatic terrain-following system.

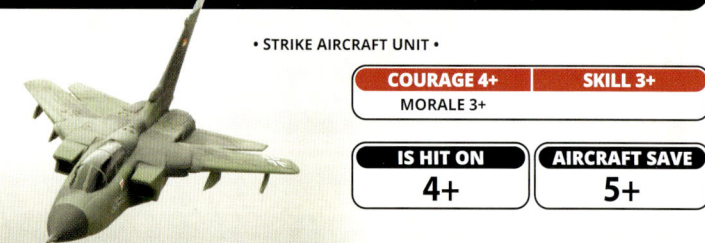

• STRIKE AIRCRAFT UNIT •

COURAGE 4+	SKILL 3+
MORALE 3+	

IS HIT ON	AIRCRAFT SAVE
4+	5+

TACTICAL	TERRAIN DASH	CROSS COUNTRY DASH	ROAD DASH	CROSS
— UNLIMITED —				AUTO

WEAPON	RANGE	ROF HALTED	ROF MOVING	ANTI-TANK	FIRE-POWER	NOTES
MW-1 submunition dispenser with KB44 bomblet	6"/15CM	SALVO		8	3+	
Mauser BK-27 auto-cannon	8"/20CM	-	3	7	5+	Anti-helicopter

The Tornado is armed with two internally mounted 27mm Mauser BK-27 auto-cannons and two AIM-9 Sidewinder missiles for self-defence. It can carry a variety of conventional bombs, as well as the MW-1 submunition dispenser that drops a variety of munitions, including the KB44 anti-tank bomblet.

DANISH BASING & PAINTING

BASING DANISH INFANTRY

Formation Command G3 rifle team

Base the Commander on a small base with a radio operator and rifleman.

Carl Gustav anti-tank team

Base Carl Gustav anti-tank teams on a medium base. Teams combine a Carl Gustav anti-tank gunner and three riflemen.

MG3 team with M72 LAW anti-tank

Base Danish Infantry teams on a medium base. Teams combine a machine-gunner, and three riflemen armed with rifles and light anti-tank weapons. Unit Leaders replace the machine-gun and a rifleman with an officer and radio operator.

Redeye AA missile team

Base Redeye AA missile teams on a large base with three AA missile gunners and three rifle-armed assistants.

DANISH TANKS

- GOLDEN OLIVE 857
- KHAKI 988
- BLACK GREY 862

105

Danish Infantry

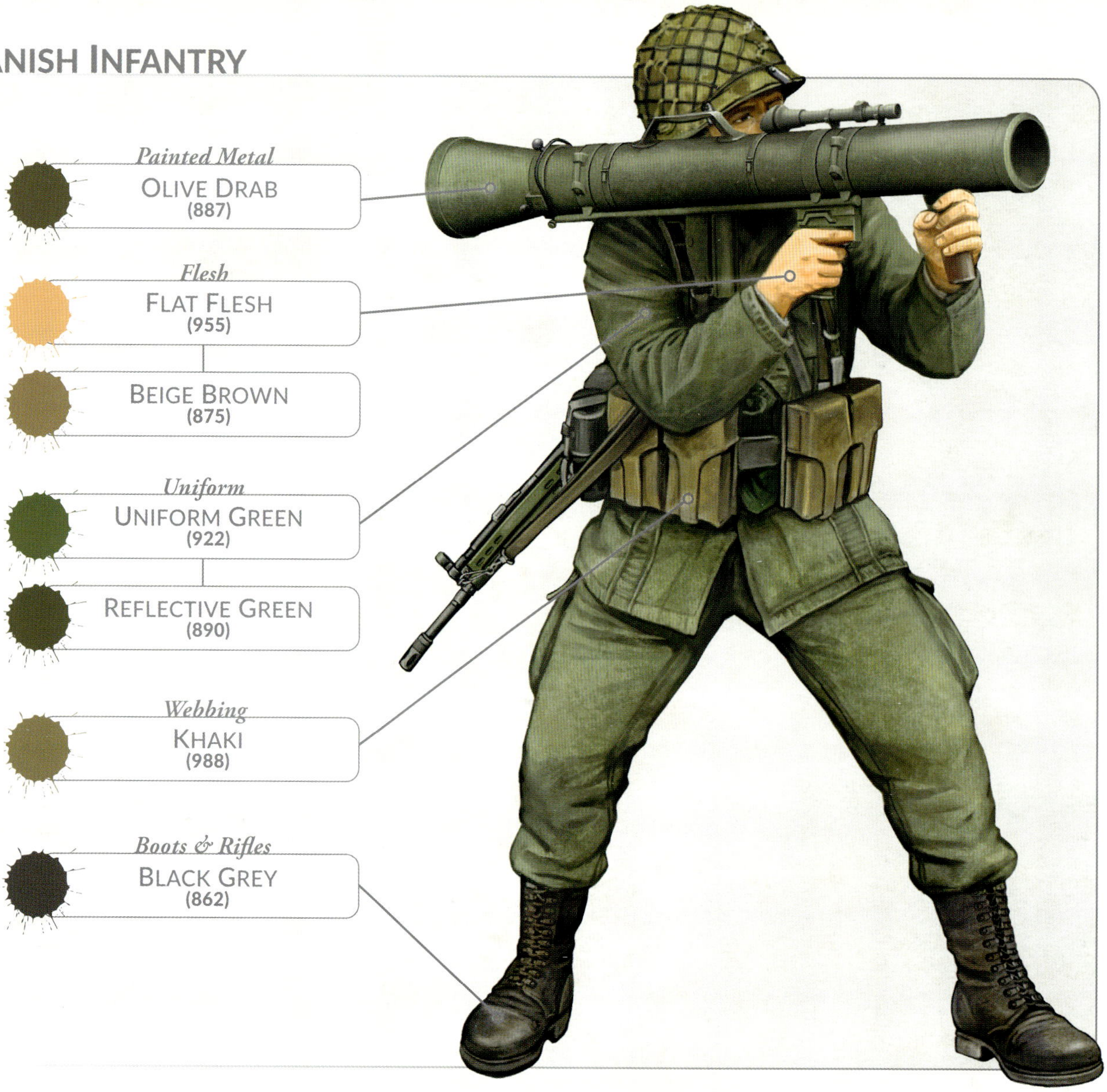

- *Painted Metal* — Olive Drab (887)
- *Flesh* — Flat Flesh (955)
- Beige Brown (875)
- *Uniform* — Uniform Green (922)
- Reflective Green (890)
- *Webbing* — Khaki (988)
- *Boots & Rifles* — Black Grey (862)

West German Aircraft

- Olive Green (967)
- Pastel Green (885)
- Field Blue (964)
- Black Grey (862)
- Olive Drab (887)

SCENARIOS

As well as playing the missions in the World War III: Team Yankee rulebook, or downloaded from the website *www.Team-Yankee.com*, you can also play scenarios inspired by your imagination, your favourite WWIII fiction, or even historical battles put into a WWIII context.

The following three scenarios are based on the actions of the Finnish, Swedish, and Norwegian forces featured in this book.

You can play them as a one-off action or in order, using the Consequences and Campaign sections to carry forward the results from one game to another. You can swap sides and play through the campaign to compare your forces and your approaches.

There is also no reason why you can't play all the scenarios with different forces. You can even try different terrain arrangements, as terrain can often make all the difference to how a game plays, or even a different sized table if you have one.

Most importantly of all, have fun and feel free to modify the scenarios anyway you see fit.

PLAYING THE CAMPAIGN WITH ONE NATION

You may like to pick your favourite Nation from this book and run them as the Nordic side in all of the scenarios. In this case use the Alternative Forces points value at the bottom of the suggetsed forces for each Scenario.

SCENARIOS SPECIAL RULES

FOG OF WAR

In a Scenario being played with the Fog Of War rule the Defender does not deploy their Units at the start of the game, but instead gets two Unit Markers (the same size as a Ranged In marker) for each Unit in their Force. Each marker should be marked as a Tank Unit or an Infantry Unit set by the type of Unit that generated it, and each token given a unique number. For example, an Infantry Unit would produce two Infantry Unit markers, numbered I1 and I2. Attachments do not generate a marker, but are instead deployed with their parent Unit.

Once the markers are generated, each Unit is allocated to a marker of the appropriate type and a record is kept of this. All markers are retained, both those with Units allocated and those without.

When the Defender deploys they place all of their markers as instructed by the Mission or Scenario instead of placing their Units on table. Unit markers are treated as Teams for the purpose of enemy Spearhead, Tactical, and Dash movement.

Once the game begins, any time an Attacker's Unit comes within 24"/60cm and Line of Sight of a Defender's Unit marker the Defender must reveal whether the marker is a Unit or not:

- If the Unit marker is allocated to a Unit, the Unit Leader is placed on the marker and its remaining Teams are placed in Command. If the Unit has an attachment, it can either be placed within 6"/15cm of its parent Unit, or anywhere in the Defender's deployment area as long as it is more that 16"/40cm from Attacking teams.
- In the Defender's turn, the Defender may chose to reveal any Unit Marker in the starting step when you would normally reveal Ambushes.
- If the Unit Marker is not allocated to a Defender's Unit, the Unit marker is simply removed from the table.

Unit Markers cannot move.

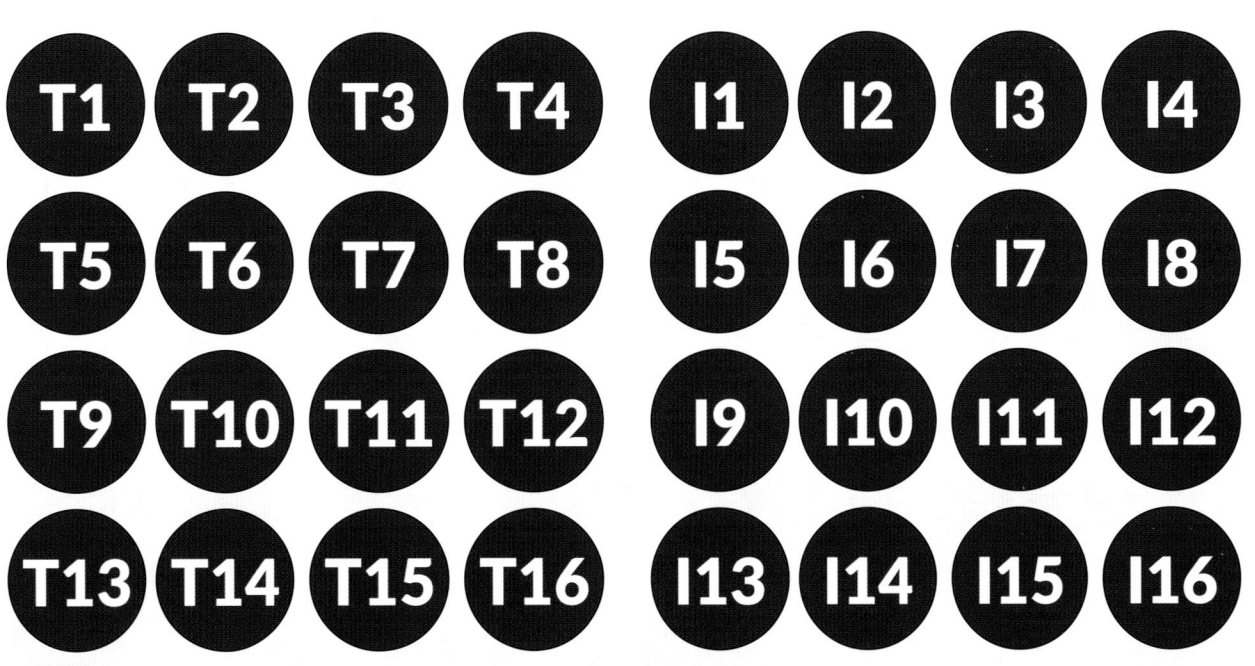

ON THE FRONTIER

Antti scrambled up to the fallen log at the top of the embankment overlooking the forestry track. The musk of the damp soil permeated his senses as he carefully rested his APILAS anti-tank weapon on the mossy bark of the log. Further along the embankment Erno had taken up position watching the gentle bend in the track. After waiting quietly for 10 minutes or so, Erno signalled Antti to ready his weapon, a Russian tank approached, range 300 metres.

Antti prepared his weapon, following the steps he had trained to do many times. The roar of the tank engine got louder; then it appeared around the bend in the track, sliding as it turned. Keeping low behind the log Antti waited for it to pass his position. He then popped up and fired the APILAS as the tank got further up the track. The grenade hit the tank in the rear with a loud crack and a massive billowing of smoke and debris. He did not have time to admire his handy work, Erno had tapped him on the shoulder, it was time to beat a hasty retreat into the forest before the rest of the enemy column turned up.

The Finnish Player is to delay the advancing Soviets, giving their main force time to deploy in strong defensive position.

The Soviet Player's force is to push through the Finnish frontier troops and on to the local town and transport hub connecting road and rail links westward.

SPECIAL RULES
- Dawn (see Page 93 of *World War III: Team Yankee*)
- Fog of War (Finnish Player, see page 107)
- Open Woods (Terrain, see below)

SETTING UP
Lay out the terrain on a 6' x 4' (180cm x 120cm) table as shown on the map on the following page. The terrain is heavily forested with woods or similar covering the table. Treat the parts of the table not covered with other types of terrain as Open Woods (see below).

Place an Objective on each of the spots marked .

OPEN WOODS
Open Woods provide concealment for teams inside the terrain. However, Line of Sight to a target team is Blocked if it is more than 2"/5cm through Open Wood terrain, unless the Range is 12"/30cm or less.

Open Woods are Tall terrain. Teams at the edge of a Open Wood are Concealed. Dash movement must be at Terrain Dash speed.

Unlike Woods, Open Wood do not require a Cross Test.

DEPLOYMENT
The Finnish player allocates Units to Unit markers and then deploys their Unit markers in the Finnish Deployment area marked on the table map using the Fog of War special rule (see page 107).

The Finnish Player places their Ranged In marker for their 120mm Mortar Platoon.

Finnish Infantry Teams may start the game in Foxholes (see page 35, 48, and 54 of *World War III: Team Yankee*).

The Soviet Force is then deployed on the table in the Soviet deployment area.

STARTING THE GAME
The Soviet Player has the first turn.

The game starts in Darkness using the Dawn rules to determine when Daylight arrives (see Page 93 of World War III: Team Yankee).

WINNING THE GAME
The Soviet Player wins if they start their turn within 4"/10cm of an Objective and end their turn with no Defending Finnish teams within 4"/10cm of that Objective.

The Finnish Player wins if they end a turn on or after the sixth turn with no Attacking Soviet Tank, Infantry, or Gun teams within 8"/20cm of the Objectives.

CONSEQUENCES
If the Soviet player wins, they have broken through the delaying position and pushed on towards the main Finnish defensive line. If the Finnish player wins they have delayed the Soviet advance, allowing their defensive position to be fully prepared.

WHAT HAPPENED
Having fought against three days of Finnish delaying actions, the Soviets finally breakthough and push on towards northern Sweden and Norway on 7 August 1985. The Soviets bring up second line units to tie down the Finnish defence forces while the main Soviet thrust aims to knock Sweden and Norway out of the war, or at least seize Norway's north, thereby freeing up the main sea route from the Kola Peninsula to the North Sea.

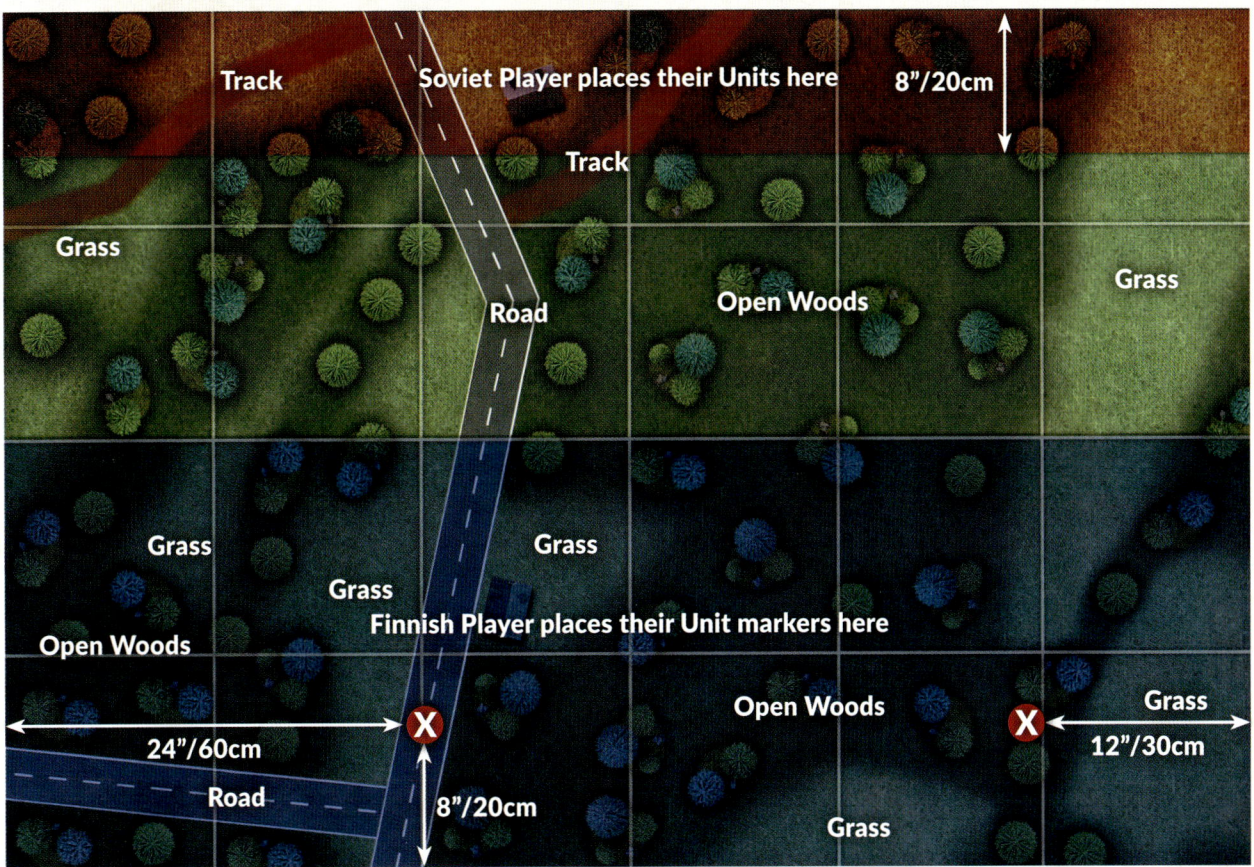

FORCES

FINNISH BTR-60 JÄÄKÄRI COMPANY

BTR-60 Jääkäri Company HQ
   1x RK 62 team
   1x BTR-60

BTR-60 Jääkäri Platoon
   7x KK 62 MG team with 66 KES 75 anti-tank
   2x APILAS anti-tank team
   4x BTR-60

BTR-60 Jääkäri Platoon
   7x KK 62 MG team with 66 KES 75 anti-tank
   2x APILAS anti-tank team
   4x BTR-60

95 S 58-61 Anti-tank Platoon
   3x 95 S 58-61 recoilless rifle
   1x APILAS anti-tank team

120mm Mortar Platoon
   3x 120mm KRH 73 mortar

T72fm1 Armoured Platoon
   3x T-72FM1

ALTERNATIVE FORCE: 51 POINTS

SOVIET MOTOR RIFLE REGIMENT

BMP Motor Rifle Battalion HQ
   1x AK-74 assault rifle team & 1x BMP-1

BMP-1 Motor Rifle Company
   7x AK-74 team with RPG-18 anti-tank
   6x RPG-7 anti-tank team
   2x PKM LMG team
   9x BMP-1

BMP-1 Motor Rifle Company
   7x AK-74 team with RPG-18 anti-tank
   6x RPG-7 anti-tank team
   2x PKM LMG team
   9x BMP-1

BMP-2 Recon Platoon
   4x BMP-2

2S1 Carnation SP Howitzer Battery
   3x 2S1 Carnation

T-62M Tank Battalion
   1x T-62M

T-62M Tank Company
   7x T-62M

T-62M Tank Company
   7x T-62M

T-62M Tank Company
   7x T-62M

ALTERNATIVE FORCE: 100 POINTS

HOLD AND FLANK

Smoke wafted across the road as Sven's Strv 103 S-Tank turned into some fields and past a collection of farm buildings. His platoon has been sitting behind the main position waiting to lend a hand where they may be needed. A radio call had prompted the company into action about 15 minutes after the sounds of battle had begun.

Just as he was approaching a small copse of trees, a turreted tank emerged out from behind the farm building to his left. His driver/gunner halted the tank, and begun swinging it around to bring its 105mm gun to bear. Sven took aim and fired the tank's gun. A few seconds later the autoloader had cycled a fresh round into the breech, but Sven's first round had hit its mark.

Three Soviet motor rifle divisions have punched through the Finnish defences in the north of Finland. On 7 August they crossed the Finno-Swedish border around Övertorneå, forcing their way across the Torne River into Sweden. As they began to push their way into Norrbotton County, they began to encounter heavily mined roads and fields. One forward detachment found itself channelled towards a narrow gap between two lakes at the village of Lombheden. Here a carefully laid Swedish ambush waited.

SPECIAL RULES

- Ambush (Swedish Player, see page 85 of *World War III: Team Yankee*)
- Immediate Reserves (Swedish Player, see page 86 of *World War III: Team Yankee*)
- Minefields (Swedish Player, see page 94 of *World War III: Team Yankee*)
- Open Woods (Terrain, See page 108)

SETTING UP

Lay out the terrain on a 6' x 4' (180cm x 120cm) table as shown on the map on the following page. Treat the parts of the table not covered in other types of terrain as Open Woods (see page 108).

Place two Objectives on the spots marked .

Place Minefield markers on the spots marked .

The Soviet player places Ranged In markers.

DEPLOYMENT

The Swedish player holds the Pvrbv 551 Anti-tank Missile Platoon and Pvpjtgb 90mm Anti-tank Platoon in Ambush. The Units under the Reserves heading will arrive from Immediate Reserves along the Swedish right long table edge within 36"/90cm of the Swedish right table corner. The remainder of the Swedish force is deployed on table in the Swedish Deployment area marked on the table map.

The Soviet force is then deployed on the table in the Soviet Deployment area.

All Swedish Infantry Teams may start the game in Foxholes (see page 35, 48, and 54 of *World War III: Team Yankee*).

SOVIET MOTOR RIFLES

The Soviet divisions earmarked to fight across the north of Scandinavia were mounted in unarmoured tracked carriers for their superior mobility across swamps and snow, instead of BMPs or BTRs. These units would dismount before engaging. Do not field these Units' Transport Attachment in this game.

STARTING THE GAME

The Soviet Player has first turn.

WINNING THE GAME

The Soviet Player wins if they start their turn within 4"/10cm of an Objective and end their turn with no Defending Swedish teams within 4"/10cm of that Objective.

The Swedish Player wins if they end a turn on or after the sixth turn with no Attacking Soviet Tank, Infantry, or Gun teams within 8"/20cm of the Objectives.

CAMPAIGN

If the Soviet player won *On the Frontier*, the Swedish player does not have time to fully prepare their defence. The Pvrbv 551 Anti-tank Missile Platoon is not placed in Ambush. It is instead deployed on the table with the other Swedish units.

If the Nordic player won *On the Frontier*, the Soviet player must play *Hold and Flank* without one T-55AM Tank Company unit.

CONSEQUENCES

If the Soviet player wins, they have broken through the Swedish counterattack, forcing them to withdraw towards Boden. If the Swedish player wins they have held off the Soviet thrust towards Boden, forcing the Soviets to redirect their attack around their position, buying time to the Swedish defence.

WHAT HAPPENED

The Soviets soon found the Swedes a tough nut to crack. Their push into northern Sweden became bogged down against continious counterattacks, and a well-organised defence. When several Soviet amphibious landings were repulsed along the Swedish Baltic coast they were finally forced to establish defensive positions across northern Sweden, screening the Swedes off as they concentrated on their push into Norway and dealing with the rallying Finns.

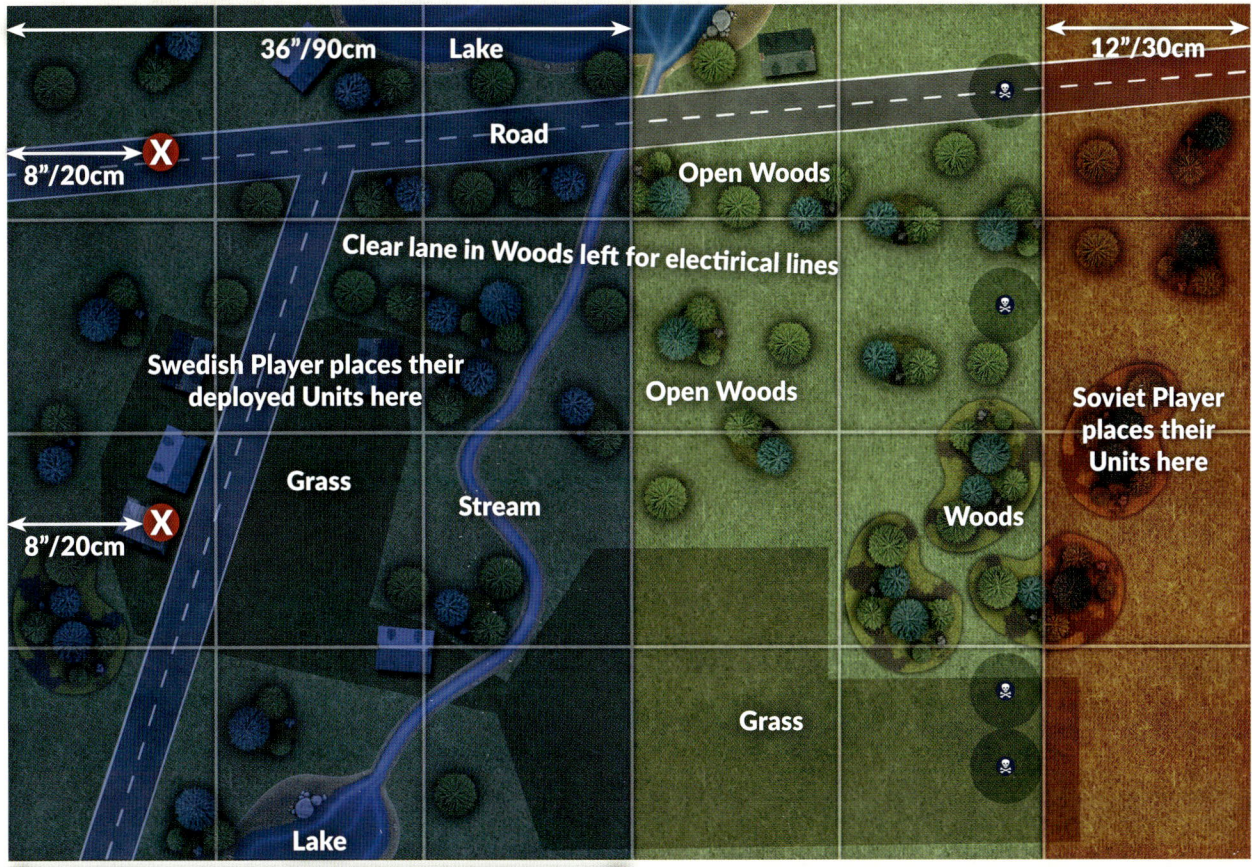

FORCES

SWEDISH MECHANISED BATTALION

Armoured Rifle Company HQ
- 1x AK4 rifle team
- 1x Pbv 302

Pbv 302 Armoured Rifle Platoon
- 3x Ksp-58 MG team
- 2x Grg m/48 anti-tank team
- 1x RBS-56 BILL missile team
- 3x Pbv 302

Pbv 302 Armoured Rifle Platoon (as above)

Pbv 302 Armoured Rifle Platoon (as above)

Ikv 91 Tracked Anti-tank Platoon
- 3x Ikv 91

IN AMBUSH

Pvrbv 551 Anti-tank Missile Platoon
- 3x Pvrbv 551

Pvpjtgb 90mm Anti-tank Platoon
- 4x 90mm Pvpjtgb

IMMEDIATE RESERVES

Strv 103 S-Tank Tank Company HQ
- 2x Strv 103 S-Tank

Strv 103 S-Tank Tank Platoon
- 3x Strv 103 S-Tank

Strv 103 S-Tank Tank Platoon
- 3x Strv 103 S-Tank

ALTERNATIVE FORCE: 77 POINTS

SOVIET MOTOR RIFLE REGIMENT

T-55AM Tank Battalion HQ
- 1x T-55AM

T-55AM Tank Company
- 8x T-55AM

T-55AM Tank Company
- 8x T-55AM

T-55AM Tank Company
- 8x T-55AM

ZSU-23-4 Shilka AA Platoon
- 4x ZSU-23-4 Shilka

2s1 Carnation SP Howitzer Battery
- 6x 2s1 Carnation

BTR-60 Motor Rifle Battalion HQ
- 1x AK-74 assault rifle team

BTR-60 Motor Rifle Company
- 10x AK-74 team with RPG-18 anti-tank
- 9x RPG-7 anti-tank team
- 1x PKM LMG team
- 2x AT-4 Spigot missile team

BTR-60 Motor Rifle Company
- 10x AK-74 team with RPG-18 anti-tank
- 9x RPG-7 anti-tank team
- 1x PKM LMG team
- 2x AT-4 Spigot missile team

Spandrel Anti-tank Platoon
- 3x Spandrel

2s3 Acacia Heavy SP Howitzer Battery
- 3x 2s3 Acacia

ALTERNATIVE FORCE: 94 POINTS

MOUNTAIN PASS

Arne and Dag jogged along the animal trail, their MG3 held over their shoulders between them, through the low scrub that clung to gentle slopes of the valley with mountains dominating either side. Behind them Håkon and Ivar carried more ammo, their G3 rifles and some LAW anti-tank weapons.

The main highway linking Northern Norway with Finland ran down the valley to the small town and fjord that sat at its foot. Several streams ran off the mountains, before converging to run down the valley. A series of defensive lines ran across the valleys and mountains, the Norwegians were well-prepared for whatever the Soviets threw at them.

The team jumped down into their position when they arrived, and quickly set up their machine-gun. Their little fortress overlooked the low scrub from a slightly elevated position so they could detect any movement through the concealment. They could also see the road running up the valley. They settled in to wait for the enemy they knew was on its way.

The Soviets have advanced across Finnish Lapland and Norwegian Finmark and are about to launch their assault on the mountain passes into central Norway and to the coast.

The Norwegians are ready, having built extensive defences in the mountains passes and valleys across the narrowest part of their country.

SPECIAL RULES

- Ambush (Norwegians, see page 85 in *World War III: Team Yankee*)
- Deep Immediate Reserves (Norwegians, see page 86 in *World War III: Team Yankee*)
- Minefields (Norwegians, see page 94 in *World War III: Team Yankee*)

SETTING UP

Lay out the terrain on a 6' x 4' (180cm x 120cm) table as shown on the map on the following page.

Place two Soviet Objectives on the spots marked .

Place Minefield markers on the spots marked .

Both Players place Ranged In markers.

TERRAIN

The areas of the table not covered by other types of terrain are covered by low shrubs, saplings and other light vegetation.

Low Shrubs and Saplings provide concealment for Teams inside the terrain. However, Line of Sight to a target Team is Blocked if it is more than 2"/5cm through Low Shrubs and Saplings terrain, unless the Range is 12"/30cm or less.

Low Shrubs and Saplings is Short Terrain. Teams at the edge of Low Shrubs and Saplings are Concealed. Dash movement must be at Terrain Dash speed.

Low Shrubs and Saplings terrain does not require a Cross Test.

DEPLOYMENT

The Norwegian player holds the NM142 Anti-tank Troop in Ambush. The Units under the Reserves heading will arrive from Deep Immediate Reserves along the Norwegian table edge. The remainder of the Norwegian force is deployed on the table in the Norwegian Deployment area marked on the table map.

The Soviet force is then deployed on the table in the Soviet Deployment area.

All Norwegian Infantry Teams may start the game in Foxholes (see page 35, 48, and 54 of *World War III: Team Yankee*).

STARTING THE GAME

The Soviet Player has the first turn.

WINNING THE GAME

The Soviet player wins if they start their turn with a Tank or Infantry Team within 4"/10cm of an Objective, and end it with no Norwegian Tank or Infantry Teams within 4"/10cm of that Objective.

The Norwegian player wins if they end a turn on or after the sixth turn with no Soviet Tank or Infantry teams within 8"/20cm of the Objectives.

CAMPAIGN

If the Soviet player won *Hold and Flank*, the Soviet player adds a T-72 Tank Company of three T-72 tanks that arrives from Immediate Reserves (see page 101 of *World War III: Team Yankee*) from the Soviet table edge.

If the Nordic player won *Hold and Flank*, the Norwegian player adds a fourth Unit of four Leopard 1 tanks to the Reserves part of their Force.

CONSEQUENCES

If the Norwegian player wins, they have stopped the Soviet's advance down the valley towards the fjord and its access to the sea. If the Soviet player wins they have pushed through the Norwegian positions and have made it to the coast, putting them in striking distance of several ports.

WHAT HAPPENED

The Norwegians slowed the pace of the Soviet advance. NATO reinforcements were able to take up defensive positions at various bottlenecks along Norway's mountainous northern coastline, hindering the Soviet's attempt to establish a hold on any of the ports they were attempting to utilise.

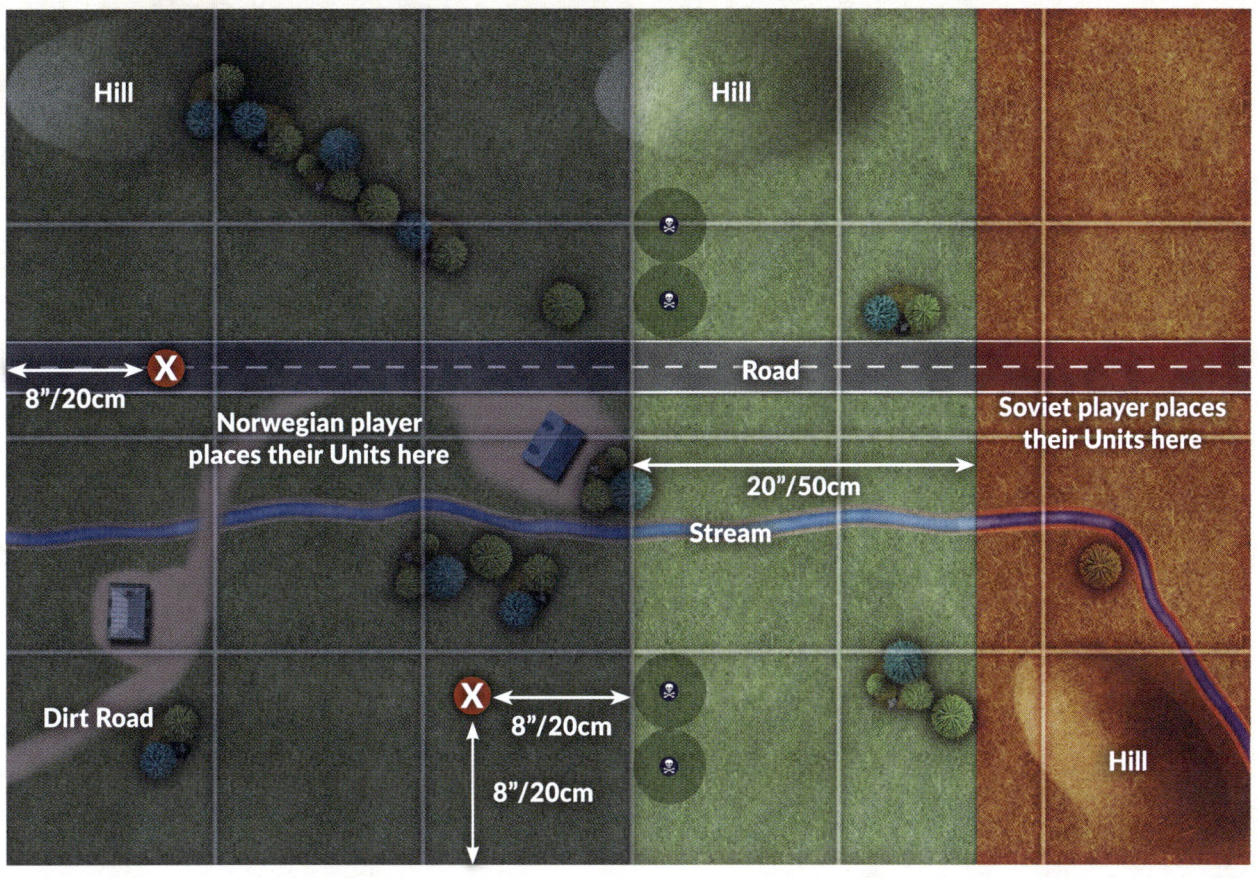

FORCES

NORWEGIAN M113 STORM SQUADRON

M113 Storm Squadron HQ
    1x AG3 rifle team
    1x NM135
M113 Storm Troop
    4x MG3 team with M72 LAW anti-tank
    3x Carl Gustav anti-tank team
    2x M113, 2x NM135
M113 Storm Troop
    (As Above)
M113 Storm Troop
    (As Above)
NM142 Anti-tank Troop (Ambush)
    4x NM142
Leopard 1 Tank Troop
    4x Leopard 1
M106 107mm Mortar Troop
    4x M106 107mm

DEEP IMMEDIATE RESERVES

Leopard 1 Tank Squadron HQ
    1x Leopard 1
Leopard 1 Tank Troop
    4x Leopard 1
Leopard 1 Tank Troop
    4x Leopard 1
NM142 Anti-tank Troop
    4x NM142

ALTERNATIVE FORCE: 79 POINTS

T-72 TANK BATTALION

T-72 Tank Battalion HQ
    1x T-72
T-72 Tank Company
    6x T-72
T-72 Tank Company
    6x T-72
BRDM-2 Recon Platoon
    4x BRDM-2
BTR-60 Motor Rifle Company
    7x AK-74 team with RPG-18 anti-tank
    6x RPG-7 anti-tank team
    1x PKM LMG team
    8x BTR-60
2s1 Carnation SP Howitzer Battery
    3x 2s1 Carnation
BMP-1 Observation Post
    1x BMP-1 OP
Mi-24 Hind Assault Helicopter Company
    2x Mi-24 Hind

ALTERNATIVE FORCE: 82 POINTS

SCENARIOS

113

CENTURION (STRV 104 & DK)

The British Centurion was one of the most widely exported tanks of the Cold War, seeing service with many of the smaller NATO national armies as well as the British. Two notable users were the Danes and the Swedes, both using the Centurion tank into the 1980s. Both nations upgraded and modernised their Centurions to keep them in service alongside their other tanks such as the Leopard 1 and Strv 103 S-Tank. These upgrades resulted in the Danish Centurion DK and the Swedish Strv 104 Centurion.

Centurion (Strv 104 & DK)

Crew:	4 - commander, gunner, loader, driver
Weight:	51 to 54 tonnes
Length:	9.75m (31' 8")
Width:	3.4m (11')
Height:	3.22m (10' 5")
Weapons:	105mm Royal Ordnance L7A3 L/52 rifled gun (Strv 104) 2x 7.62mm MG (DK) 1x 7.62mm MG, 1x 12.7mm MG
Armour:	Steel 51-152mm Strv 101R, 102R, & 104 adds Explosive Reactive Armour
Speed:	(Strv 104) 50km/h (35 mph) (DK) 35km/h (22 mph)
Engine:	(Strv 104) Teledyne Continental AVDS 1790 2DC V12 750 hp (560 kW) (DK) V12-cylinder Rolls-Royce Meteor Mk IV B. 650 hp (485 kW)
Range:	(Strv 104) 480 km (300 miles) (DK) 100 km (62 miles)

- The Danish Centurion DK is armed with the 105mm L7 gun without a thermal sleeve, while the Swedish Strv 104 Centurion has a thermal sleeve fitted to its gun.
- The Swedish Strv 104 Centurion is also fitted with Explosive Reactive Armour (ERA) blocks, while the Danish Centurion DK is not.
- The Danish Centurions retain the original Rolls-Royce Meteor engine, but the Swedish Strv 104 Centurion has a different engine deck because of its new American Continental engine.

6' / 1.8m

The Swedes first considered purchasing British Centurion tanks in 1950, but the British were unable to supply to Sweden at that time due to their own requirements. However, after the Swedes considered and trialed a number of French AMX designs, the British agreed to supply Centurions to the Swedes between 1953 and 1954. The first Centurions to arrive were Centurion Mk.3 (designated Strv 81) armed with the 20 pdr (84mm) main gun. By 1956 the Swedes had over 400 Strv 81 Centurions (Mk.3 or 5). In 1958 they purchased 110 Centurion Mk.10 tanks which they designated Strv 101. These were armed with a 105mm L7 gun, had a more powerful engine, and increased frontal armour to 120mm. Between 1964 and 1966 the older Strv 81 were upgraded to the same standard as the Strv 101, designated as the Strv 102, so all their Centurions were armed with the 105mm L7 gun.

The next modernisation began in 1973 and continued until 1983. General refurbishment, electronics updates and the addition of a laser range-finder increased the service life of these vehicles radically. Further upgrades began in 1983 with external changes such as lights, a pair of mortars added to the roof, and the addition of explosive reactive armour (ERA), similar to the kind developed by the Israeli RAFAEL company as Blazer. These were designated Strv 101R and 102R.

The final Swedish upgrade to their Centurions was the Strv 104 which fitted improved ERA armour, a thermal sleeve for the gun, and replaced the original transmission and engine with those of the American M60, tank improving its mobility and range substantially.

The Danes initally received Centurion Mk.3 tanks as part of the Mutual Defense Aid Program in 1953, some of them veterans of the Korean War. In 1954 the Besa MG was replaced with a Browning 7.62mm MG and was designated the Centurion Mk V. In 1959 a 12.7mm Browning AA MG was mounted on the turret.

In 1964 106 tanks were modified with the British 105mm L7 gun, and the 7.62mm Browning was replaced by the German MG3 (Mk V, 2). 90 tanks were further upgraded with a laser range-finder and night vision equipment in 1985 (Mk V, 2 DK or DK for short).

However, a number of Centurion Mk.3 still armed with 20 pdr (84mm) guns continued to served in the Danish anti-tank tank battalions supporting the infantry.